CYCLING THE
WAY OF THE ROSES

About the Author

Rachel Crolla is lucky enough to live a few miles from the Way of the Roses. Her early biking memories include learning the hard way how to ride up the local hills on a single-speed BMX. Having lived and cycled all her life in the White Rose county, she was thrilled to write about places which are close to her heart. Rachel started out touring on hybrid bikes, completing rides such as the Coast to Coast (C2C) and a version of the Walney to Wear (W2W). She then explored some of the region's excellent mountain-biking terrain but in recent years has become a convert to road cycling, in which she admits to having a slow and steady approach.

As well as spending time in the saddle, Rachel also enjoys hillwalking, rock-climbing and scrambling. In 2007, she became the first woman to climb the highest peak in every country in Europe. She has worked as an outdoor writer and photographer on three other Cicerone guides.

Other Cicerone guides by the author

Scrambles in Snowdonia (with Steve Ashton and Carl McKeating)
Walking in the Auvergne (with Carl McKeating)
Europe's High Points (with Carl McKeating)

CYCLING THE
WAY OF THE ROSES

COAST TO COAST ACROSS LANCASHIRE AND YORKSHIRE, WITH SIX CIRCULAR DAY RIDES

by Rachel Crolla

JUNIPER HOUSE, MURLEY MOSS,
OXENHOLME ROAD, KENDAL, CUMBRIA LA9 7RL
www.cicerone.co.uk

© Rachel Crolla 2018
First edition 2018
ISBN: 978 1 85284 912 2

Printed in China on behalf of Latitude Press Ltd
A catalogue record for this book is available from the British Library.

Route mapping by Lovell Johns www.lovelljohns.com
© Crown copyright 2018 OS PU100012932.
NASA relief data courtesy of ESRI

All photography by Rachel Crolla and Carl McKeating.

Updates to this Guide

While every effort is made by our authors to ensure the accuracy of guidebooks as they go to print, changes can occur during the lifetime of an edition. Any updates that we know of for this guide will be on the Cicerone website (www.cicerone.co.uk/912/updates), so please check before planning your trip. We also advise that you check information about such things as transport, accommodation and shops locally. Even rights of way can be altered over time. We are always grateful for information about any discrepancies between a guidebook and the facts on the ground, sent by email to updates@cicerone.co.uk or by post to Cicerone, Juniper House, Murley Moss, Oxenholme Road, Kendal, LA9 7RL.

Register your book: To sign up to receive free updates, special offers and GPX files where available, register your book at www.cicerone.co.uk.

Front cover: Superb cycling between the narrow dry stone walls of the road between Cracoe and Burnsall (Day 1)

CONTENTS

Acknowledgements

I'd like to thank my long-suffering partner Carl McKeating, who has done everything but write the book; riding all the routes (some several times) and even completing 'the Way in a Day' in the interests of proving that it is possible for a mere mortal. Also thanks to my children, who have supported me on lots of cycling trips and have learned to ride bikes during the writing of this book.

Some other great people have volunteered their time to help. Thanks to Scott Barnett, Angela Newton, Mike Armstrong, Beck Crolla, Chris and Harriet Truss, Paul Copley, Charlotte Hatch, Glen Thistlethwaite, Marc Harrison, Bridget and James Blanchard, Ed Clews, Malcolm McCauley and Leo Carne. I am also grateful to Richard Keeble and the team at AGH for patching up my arm after I hit some ice during a research ride. Finally thanks to the late Dave Crolla, who passed on the wisdom that 'you can never have too many bikes' and who would have loved cycling the Way of the Roses.

Passing Pen-y-ghent on the Malham Tarn detour (Day 1)

Symbols used on route maps

 route

 traffic-free section

 alternative route

 start/finish point

 start point

 finish point

 alternative start/finish point

 alternative start point

 alternative finish point

 route direction

> steep ascent or descent

≫ very steep ascent or descent

 café

 public house

 bike shop

all amenities

caution

castle or fort

church/cathedral

battlefield

point of interest

· other feature

Contour lines are drawn at 50m intervals and labelled at 100m intervals. Route maps are drawn at 1:100,000 (1cm = 1km)

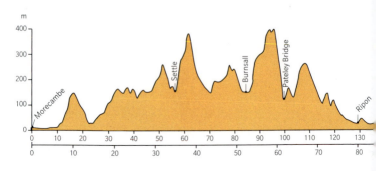

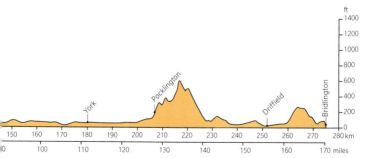

ROUTE SUMMARY TABLES

The Way of the Roses: The three-day ride

Day	Start	Finish	Distance	Ascent	Page
Day 1	Morecambe (SD 427 643)	Burnsall (SE 032 613)	53 miles (85km)	980m	42
Day 2	Burnsall (SE 032 613)	York (SE 602 523)	58 miles (93km)	1005m	66
Day 3	York (SE 602 523)	Bridlington (TA 191 675)	62 miles (100km)	450m	90

The three-day ride east to west

Day	Start	Finish	Distance	Ascent	Page
1	Bridlington (TA 191 675)	York (SE 602 523)	53 miles (85km)	450m	112
2	York (SE 602 523)	Burnsall (SE 032 613)	58 miles (93km)	1000m	88
3	Burnsall (SE 032 613)	Morecambe (SD 427 643)	62 miles (100km)	985m	65

The Way of the Roses: a four day itinerary

Day	Start	Finish	Distance	Intermediate distances	Refreshments
1	Morecambe	Settle	35 miles (56km)	Lancaster 4 miles (6km); Hornby 15 miles (24km); Clapham 25 miles (40km)	Morecambe; Lancaster; Crook o'Lune; Hornby; Wray; Clapham; Austwick
2	Settle	Ripon	43 miles (70km)	Cracoe 12 miles (19km); Appletreewick 18 miles (29km); Pateley Bridge 27 miles (44km)	Airton; Hetton; Cracoe; Burnsall; Appletreewick; Stump Cross caverns area; Pateley Bridge; Fountains Abbey
3	Ripon	Pocklington	48 miles (77km)	Boroughbridge 10 miles (16km); Linton-on-Ouse 20 miles (32km); York 31 miles (50km); Stamford Bridge 42 miles (68km)	Boroughbridge; Linton-on-Ouse; Beningbrough; York; Stamford Bridge
4	Pocklington	Bridlington	44 miles (71km)	Huggate 8 miles (13km); Hutton Cranswick 20 miles (32km); Driffield 25 miles (40km); Burton Agnes 34 miles (55km)	Millington; Kilnwick Percy; Huggate; Hutton Cranswick; Driffield; Nafferton; Harpham; Burton Agnes

The Way of the Roses: a five day itinerary

Day	Start	Finish	Distance	Intermediate distances	Refreshments
1	Morecambe	Clapham	26 miles (42km)	Lancaster 4 miles (7km); Hornby 15 miles (24km)	Lancaster; Crook o'Lune; Hornby; Wray
2	Clapham	Burnsall	26 miles (42km)	Settle 9 miles (14km)	Austwick; Settle; Airton; Hetton

11

The Way of the Roses: a five day itinerary

Day	Start	Finish	Distance	Intermediate distances	Refreshments
3	Burnsall	Ripon	36 miles (60km)	Pateley Bridge 15 miles (24km)	Burnsall; Appletreewick; Stump Cross caverns area; Pateley Bridge; Brimham Rocks; Fountains Abbey
4	Ripon	Pocklington	40 miles (64km)	Boroughbridge 10 miles (16km); York 22 miles (36km); Stamford Bridge 32 miles (51km)	Boroughbridge; York; Stamford Bridge
5	Pocklington	Bridlington (TA 191 675)	44 miles (71km)	Huggate 8 miles (13km); Hutton Cranswick 20 miles (32km); Driffield 25 miles (40km); Burton Agnes 34 miles (55km)	Millington; Kilnwick Percy; Huggate; Hutton Cranswick; Driffield; Nafferton; Harpham; Burton Agnes

The Way of the Roses: a two day itinerary

Day	Start	Finish	Distance	Intermediate distances	Refreshments
1	Morecambe	Ripon	77 miles (124km)	Lancaster 4 miles (6km); Hornby 15 miles (24km); Clapham 25 miles (40km); Settle 35 miles (56km); Cracoe 48 miles (77km); Burnsall 53 miles (85km); Pateley Bridge 64 miles (103km)	Morecambe; Lancaster; Crook o'Lune; Hornby; Wray; Clapham; Austwick; Settle; Airton; Hetton; Cracoe; Burnsall; Appletreewick; Greenhow; Pateley Bridge; Fountains Abbey
2	Ripon	Bridlington	93 miles (150km)	Boroughbridge 10 miles (16km); York 31 miles (50km); Stamford Bridge 42 miles (68km); Pocklington 50 miles (80km); Driffield 74 miles (119km)	Boroughbridge; Linton-on-Ouse; Beningbrough; York; Dunnington; Stamford Bridge; Pocklington; Millington; Huggate; Hutton Cranswick; Driffield; Burton Agnes; Bridlington

Day rides

Ride		Start/finish	Finish (if not a circuit)	Distance	Ascent
1	Arnside and Silverdale tour	Lancaster Castle (SD 473 620)		40 miles (64km)	600m
2	The Way of the Dales	Skipton Castle (SD 990 520)		49 miles (79km)	1015m
3	Brontë country and the dark satanic hills	Skipton Castle (SD 990 520)		44 miles (71km)	1430/1600m
4	Otley and Knaresborough round	Otley market place (SE 204 454)		46 miles (74km)	960m
5	Around the Wolds in a day	Huggate (SE 882 550)		47 miles (76km)	870m
6	Bridlington to Scarborough extension	Bridlington (TA 191 675)	Scarborough (TA 045 885)	26½ miles (43km)	350m

Passing the limestone scars on the slopes of Rye Loaf Hill above Settle (Day 1)

INTRODUCTION

Crossing Winterburn bridge in front of a sea of buttercups (Day 1)

The Way of the Roses will appeal to just about everyone who loves cycling. The route is a 170-mile (274km) coast-to-coast ride that opened in 2010. It was designed to link the historic Red and White Rose counties of Lancashire and Yorkshire using scenic country lanes, minor roads and traffic-free cycle paths to create a superb ride between the seaside resort towns of Morecambe in the west and Bridlington in the east. Travelling by bike across the country is a hugely satisfying objective, and cycling the Way of the Roses is a challenge within the reach of cyclists of all abilities.

The beauty of the Way of the Roses is that it works equally well for those wishing to get serious miles under their wheels in some of the best cycling territory in the UK, and also as a more leisurely tour taking in the wealth of attractive sites that are passed. There is so much to see along the route that even the most committed pedal pushers will be tempted out of their saddles.

The route lends itself to making pitstops in idyllic villages and replenishing calories in riverside tearooms. It also provides a great choice of accommodation, pubs and restaurants. Added to that is an impressive array of castles, cathedrals, abbeys and prehistoric sites, along with stunning natural features such as the Three Peaks,

Brimham Rocks and Flamborough Head; but the star attraction always remains the cycling itself.

The ride has been ingeniously designed by Sustrans, taking little-known minor roads and avoiding busy parts of towns and cities by using traffic-free paths along rivers and dismantled railways. It follows the River Lune inland through Lancaster, then starts to get more hilly as it skirts the northern reaches of the Forest of Bowland Area of Outstanding Natural Beauty (AONB) before crossing the county border into the Yorkshire Dales National Park. Here the panoramic cycling on single-track lanes between ancient dry-stone walls is one of the highlights of the route. The Way climbs over into Nidderdale (another AONB) passing Fountains Abbey, after which the hills diminish and the ride continues through Ripon and on across the arable land of the Vale of York. The Way makes a grand entrance into the historic city of York, dodging the suburbs via a riverside cycle path and emerging through the medieval city walls to the Minster courtyard. Some pristine red-stone villages and short off-road sections add interest until the ride reaches the enchanting winding valleys of the Yorkshire Wolds. Thereafter the miles fly by on a former Roman road then down to the North Beach of Bridlington and the North Sea with its spectacular coastline of Flamborough Head Cliffs.

WHY DO THE WAY OF THE ROSES?

If you are trying to decide between this ride and other coast routes – the

Approaching the marketplace in Ripon, with the Cathedral behind (Day 2)

On the road from Keasden to Clapham with Ingleborough beyond (Day 1)

C2C being the most well known – the Roses ride is much more road-bike friendly, has fewer sections on busy roads and (as of 2017) more consistent signage. Cycling the Way of the Roses can be approached as either a holiday or a challenge (or a bit of both). Average cyclists on average bikes will find it both achievable and enjoyable. It makes a perfect short active break and it's a great way to see some of Lancashire and Yorkshire's best landscapes. The start and finish points are accessible by train and the route-finding is simple. This swathe of country is a hotbed of cycling and you will find enthusiasm for the sport throughout the route, along with a warm welcome and amenities designed with cyclists in mind.

HOW TOUGH IS IT?

One of the great things about the Way of the Roses is that it is a realistically attainable goal for most people. You can make it as tough or as easy as you like; some people might want to challenge themselves to race along it in two days, while others might choose to do five shorter day sections. Having ridden the route several times and talked to different Roses riders, the general consensus seems to be that an average relatively fit cyclist doing the ride over three days will find it challenging but still enjoyable. If you can comfortably ride 50 miles (80km) with 1000m of ascent and still clamber back onto your saddle the next day, then you will be more than able to tackle the three-day itinerary. If the

Starting the toughest climb of the route up Settle's High Hill Lane (Day 1)

outcome is in any doubt, plan to take longer.

For seasoned cycle tourers, the Way of the Roses route is more or less comparable to the C2C ride further north. There is slightly less ascent on the Roses ride but the route is about 30 miles (48km) longer and your legs will feel the extra distance on the final flatter section going west to east.

There is roughly 2500m of ascent on the route, which is mainly on the western half of the ride. It therefore makes sense to have a longer, flatter final day, however you choose to break up the route. Going west to east, the steepest climb is up High Hill Lane out of Settle. This reaches 20% at the very least and is the main place on the route where cyclists – particularly heavily loaded ones – have been seen getting off to push. Travelling at an average speed of around 11mph, you might expect to spend fewer than 16 hours in the saddle for the whole route. This doesn't sound like a lot, but five hours of riding time repeated for three consecutive days has quite a cumulative effect. Also worth considering is that five hours' worth of actual pedalling does not equate to a five-hour day. Part of the fun of cycling in a group is to stop for a leisurely lunch break, and the shorter stops for map checks, photos, bike fettling, calls of nature and clothing adjustments all add up.

Other factors can come into play to make the ride tougher or easier. As most people do not have the luxury of waiting for optimal conditions and setting off at a moment's notice, cyclists will mainly be at the mercy of the elements. Of course Lancashire and Yorkshire are famed for their Mediterranean climates, but bad weather can make the ride a good percentage harder. The prevailing wind direction also plays a part. The general wisdom is that the prevailing winds are westerly, which is why the Way of the Roses is predominantly ridden from west to east. However, sod's law often overrides the general wisdom and cyclists have been known to face a torrid easterly headwind on the latter section of this route. North-easterly winds are most common in spring, particularly April or May when they can blow for days or even weeks at a time. It is best not to bank on having favourable winds and then you won't be frustrated if things don't blow your way.

LOGISTICS – GETTING THERE AND BACK

Once the decision has been taken to ride the Way of the Roses, the next step will be to work out how. There are a few options depending on location and the size of the party.

By train

For small groups and solo travellers, the train is a viable option. The advantages are that it is environmentally friendly and cyclists can set off from home and make their way back again from a different place. Morecambe is on a branch line which connects to the West Coast Mainline (at nearby Lancaster), but is also served by direct trains from Skipton and Leeds. Lancaster is well connected by rail, with direct services to Manchester, Birmingham, Glasgow

Jubilant Roses cyclists wait for their return transport after a two-day ride

and London Euston. Bridlington is on the Yorkshire Coast Line and trains go to and from Scarborough, Hull, Doncaster and Sheffield. Services to and from both Morecambe and Bridlington are operated by Northern Rail, and no reservations are needed to take bikes on these trains. The trains don't have to carry more than two bicycles at a time, if they are busy, but this seems to be down to the discretion of the staff and no problems have been reported. All UK rail operators carry accompanied bikes free of charge, but different operators on your journey may want you to reserve a space for your bike when you book your ticket.

It is possible to leave a car in Morecambe and catch a train back from Bridlington. This takes over four hours and involves changing at Hull and Leeds. The last trains allowing you to do this are not very late in the day. Alternatively, by extending the ride to Scarborough, it is possible to return to Morecambe by rail, changing once at Leeds. To work out whether the train is a viable option for your trip, check on www.nationalrail.co.uk.

With a support vehicle

For a group of up to four cyclists, this seems to be a fairly popular option. It involves persuading or paying a family member or friend (with a large car and bike rack) to drop cyclists and bikes in Morecambe and then to pick them up several days later in Bridlington. This may be more or less

attractive depending on where they live and the timescale of their ride.

Some groups have a support vehicle which meets them at overnight stops. Support vehicles are strongly discouraged from driving large sections of the route; this practice is inconsiderate to other cyclists and not in keeping with the ethos of the route. However, a considerate support vehicle could carry baggage and potentially help with equipment problems.

It is easy to find paid parking close to the start and finish points. There is long-stay parking in Morecambe just off Northumberland Street, 300 metres up the promenade from the Roses start point. In Bridlington, Beaconsfield long-stay parking is 400 metres south of the finish off Carlisle Road.

With return transport

This is a good option for larger groups of cyclists. A company transports cyclists and bikes between Bridlington and Morecambe either at the start of or end of the ride. A small number of companies organise a 'package' combining both accommodation and return transport between Bridlington and Morecambe. Details of companies currently offering these services are in Appendix B.

By bike

Some people choose to cycle from home to the start and back home from the finish of the Roses route. Most may not have the time or inclination to do this, but it is worth considering combining the Way of the Roses with another coast-to-coast route, making a round trip. This strategy works best with a return trip on a reversed version of the nearby Walney-to-Whitby ride. There are good cycling links between the two routes. Search online for the National Cycle Network map.

HOW MANY DAYS?

Although this book primarily describes the route as a three-day ride, many people choose to take four days to complete the Way of the Roses. In order to have an enjoyable three-day ride you will need to be saddle fit and have completed some training (day rides of 50 miles/80km) in the weeks leading up to your trip. A three-day ride is within the capability of an average cyclist, but there is no shame in planning to take a little longer. A four-day ride leaves a bit more room to manoeuvre in the event of inclement weather, headwinds, punctures and tired legs, as well as giving more time to travel to the start and home from the finish. It also allows for an itinerary including, for example, a visit to Fountains Abbey, York Minster and perhaps the Coldstones Cut, Brimham Rocks or Burton Agnes. Taking four days still means plenty of time in the saddle, but a comforting proportion of time in teashops too.

Those with more time on their hands who want to spend some of their cycling trip acquainting themselves with the sights and sounds of Lancashire and Yorkshire should

Immaculate topiary at Burton Agnes Hall (Day 3)

Climbing out of Millington Dale towards Pocklington (Day 1)

consider a five-day itinerary. The ride splits up nicely into five interesting sections and allows time for most of the main points of interest on route to be savoured, rather than ridden past. A five-day ride feels much more like a holiday than a challenge.

Another option for fit and strong cyclists used to riding long distances is to do the ride in two days. This would be a serious challenge for average cyclists but if time is short and fitness high then it means that the ride can be done in a weekend. The two-day itinerary works quite well breaking up the ride in Pateley Bridge or Ripon but means a much hillier first day and a longer, flatter second day. This two-day option lends itself well to strong parties who can make a relatively early start from Morecambe.

For the super-fit, it is possible to complete the whole ride as a day challenge.

The Way in three days

The Way splits up neatly into three stages: Day 1 Morecambe to Burnsall 53 miles (85km); Day 2 Burnsall to York 58 miles (94km); Day 3 York to Bridlington 62 miles (100km). The vast majority of the hills come on the first two days and the long third day is deceptively straightforward. It's worth noting that the first overnight stop is in the small Dales village of Burnsall. Further accommodation options can be found in Appletreewick, Airton, Hetton and Cracoe, or even slightly off route in Grassington.

If staying in a city like York on the second night isn't your thing, there are other ways of breaking up a three-day ride. A shorter final day allowing for onward travel on the same day would be: Morecambe to Pateley Bridge 63 miles (101km); Pateley Bridge to Pocklington 65 miles (105km); Pocklington to Bridlington 43 miles (69km). For a shorter first day try Morecambe to Settle 35 miles (56km), Settle to York 75 miles (121km), and York to Bridlington 62 miles (100km).

The Way in four days

There are two good four-day itineraries, depending on where you prefer to stop overnight. The first way is as described in the Route Summary Tables at the start of this book, breaking the route up into logical and relatively evenly matched sections. The only downside is that this doesn't allow for a stop in York. If you want to have a shorter third day and spend some time sightseeing in York, it is possible to stop there on the third night having ridden 31 miles (50km) from Ripon, leaving a longer fourth day of 61 miles (98km) to Bridlington.

The Way in five days

A five-day plan allows some flexibility and the one given in the Route Summary Tables can be easily tweaked to lengthen or shorten stages according to where sightseeing stops are made or to allow for a shorter day travelling to or from home. This itinerary is a starting point and works on the logic of shorter hillier days at the start, followed by longer flatter ones. Again, this plan does not allow for

spending a night in York. That would be ideally suited to a six-day itinerary, stopping in York and then Pocklington before reaching the East Yorkshire coast on the final day.

The Way in two days

A two-day assault on the Way of the Roses is best tackled with an overnight stop in Ripon. Although it is not halfway in terms of mileage, the area from Brimham Rocks to Ripon feels like a psychological mid-point as all the big ascents have been overcome. This gives a longer but mainly flat second day, when determination and staying in the saddle are the key to success, especially when riding with aching muscles after the

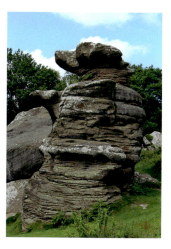

The Dancing Bear at Brimham Rocks (Day 2)

punishing ascents of the first day. Despite the extra miles on the second day and the potential of aching legs from the first day's climbs, most people actually find the second day considerably easier. Pateley Bridge is another option for the overnight break, but adding the tough climb up to Brimham to a long second day would provide an extra challenge.

THE WAY IN A DAY

Feeling on top of the world – starting the descent to Airton while cycling the Way in a Day

This is not an unrealistic goal but requires serious training and great determination. Always remember that the most important thing is to enjoy the ride, whatever happens.

The ride is much easier in decent yet not excessively hot or sunny weather, and westerly winds are a huge advantage. Make an early start; it is much harder to cycle the last section of the route in the dark when you are tired.

A super-fit cyclist with an average speed upwards of 14mph on hilly terrain will take roughly 11–13 hours in the saddle, with two additional hours of breaks (including a 30–40-minute lunch stop). Try to rope in someone in a vehicle to meet you at three points (less to carry and an incentive to reach the next stop), but be considerate and avoid having a car accompany you on stretches of the route. Take on as many calories as possible and keep hydration levels up. Eat whatever you are used to. Carry at least two water bottles and drink regularly.

Building up high mileages on endurance rides and plenty of shorter, faster rides up hills will help get you in shape. Testing yourself with a 100-mile-plus (160km) ride with over 1500m ascent will be a great psychological boost.

The stunning Dales village of Burnsall is a great overnight stop on the three-day ride (Day 1)

CYCLING THE ROUTE EAST TO WEST

Although it is described from Morecambe to Bridlington in the main part of this book, the Way of the Roses is perfectly feasible in the opposite direction. East to west might appeal for various reasons: if you have already completed the ride in the standard direction; if the logistics prove easier that way around; or if your plans are flexible and the forecast is for prevailing easterly winds.

In the main, the Way is simple to follow from east to west (Sustrans intends the route to be followed in either direction and so it is sign-posted both ways). Having said that, there are a handful of spots where the signs for cyclists travelling from Bridlington to Morecambe are missing or not as clear as the ones for the standard direction. Therefore a little more care is needed with route-finding, and even cyclists who have previously ridden the Way west to east should take care. A good strategy is to look out for the signs for both directions and scan ahead to the posts and signage at upcoming junctions. There are a few places where the east-to-west route differs slightly from the standard direction due to one-way systems in place.

In spite of the fact that British weather systems are dominated by westerly winds – aiding a west-to-east traverse of the country – there are many times when substantial easterly winds set in for days at a time, favouring those making an east-to-west journey. Plan for your ride being considerably harder and taking longer if headwinds are forecast.

On balance the Way of the Roses is a more enjoyable outing done from west to east. Starting from Morecambe, the flatter and lengthier third section can be done with tired legs on the third day. Those starting from Bridlington should note that all the harder ascents come on the second half of the route, when energy levels may have declined. That is not to say that the east-to-west option does not have its merits.

WHERE TO STAY

There is ample accommodation along the route, wherever you choose to break up the ride, and a detailed list is given in Appendix A. Many people choose the option of staying in B&B accommodation – this is reasonably priced and saves cyclists the hassle of finding their own breakfast (though be warned that fry-ups and serious hills don't always mix well!). Those who prefer pub accommodation will find plenty of choice; breakfast is often included and evening meals and drinks easily available. The cheapest options include basic bunkhouses – a number of these are convenient for the route. They are well worth considering if you want to cut costs by sharing dorm-style rooms or have a large group. Some cycle tourers choose to load their bikes with camping equipment. There is a satisfaction in carrying all you need,

and campsites are by far the cheapest option. However, if choosing this option put in some practice cycling a good distance with a heavily loaded bike. Some quirkier accommodation options are included in Appendix A: a village hall, a yurt – and even a treehouse.

WHAT KIND OF BIKE?

The answer to this question is simple: use a bike that you are comfortable riding and with which you are familiar. Exactly what type of bike is less important. Don't be tempted to borrow a friend's bike that doesn't fit you and hasn't been serviced. Likewise, a bike that has stood unused for years in the shed is unlikely to be reliable. For a successful long-distance ride, worry less about the type of bike and more about whether it is in good condition.

If there are limits to your mechanical expertise, then it is well worth taking your bike to the local shop for a pre-Roses service. Against the cost – which might only be £20 if everything is in order – weigh up the inconvenience of having to do any major running repairs en route or having to quit the ride. Make sure that the bike is set up correctly for you – you will be on it for long consecutive stretches. Incorrectly positioned saddles, handlebars and shifters can all make life far more difficult. Again, take your bike to your local cycle shop if it doubt.

Road bikes

Many would-be Roses riders are worried by the mention of off-road sections on the route and wonder whether they will cope on a road bike. Rest assured, the Way of the Roses is designed so that it can be done on a road bike, and the vast majority of people do just that. Even the bumpiest short section (on a dirt track near Stamford Bridge) is in no way beyond the capabilities of any serviceable road bike. The sections on narrow cycle paths will slow you down, but if your only reason for doing the Way of the Roses is to get a fast time, then perhaps the ride is not for you. The dropped handlebars of road bikes enable cyclists to vary their position and be more aerodynamic on flat and downhill stretches.

For years, road bikes had 23mm or even skinnier tyres, but the most popular choice now seems to be 25mm. This is suitable for riding the Roses route where there are many less-than-perfect road surfaces and some gravel tracks. The 25mm tyres give a good balance between comfort, likelihood of getting punctures and speed. Some aerodynamics experts believe that slightly wider tyres used on road bikes could actually be faster than skinny ones. There are also

Crossing the Lune Viaduct on a hybrid bike, with the Crook o' Lune beyond (Day 1)

28mm tyres that are becoming more common for road bikes too.

There is not room in this book to open up the can of worms that constitutes the technicalities of gearing. A debate about the precise number of cogs on your bike's cassette and whether a double or triple chainring is optimal is best left to cycling magazines. If you have been riding your bike to get saddle fit for the Way of the Roses, then you know what sort of gradient you feel comfortable tackling. There is always a more expensive, higher spec bike out there but this ride should not be beyond the scope of a reasonably fit person on any good-quality entry-level bike. I have ridden the Way on a 16-speed road bike and still managed to stay in the saddle on all the hills.

Endurance road bikes such as those aimed at sportive riders and adventure models such as gravel bikes are gaining popularity at the time of writing and are undoubtedly suitable for riding the Way of the Roses if money is no object. Adventure bikes are a variation on the traditional touring bike: basically a sturdy road bike that may be set up for use with panniers, mudguards and wider tyres.

Hybrid bikes

These are also a good choice for this route. I have ridden the Way of the Roses on both a road bike with 25mm tyres and a hybrid and have come across groups of cyclists with members on both kinds of bikes. A hybrid was slower overall, but the hills were easier and the ride fractionally more comfortable. It is a matter of personal choice. Despite the vast numbers of lycra-clad road bikers around, sales of hybrid bikes are still very high because these bikes are good all-rounders – the sturdy frames and wider tyres are great for tackling canal towpaths and gritty road surfaces.

Tandems

Tandems are a relatively common sight on the Way of the Roses. Although some tandems deviate from the main route to avoid the steeper climbs and descents, experienced tandemists should be able to stay in the saddle with one or two exceptions. Bear in mind that the unsurfaced section near Stamford Bridge may be tricky on a heavily loaded tandem. There are very few narrow traffic stopper posts and gates that have to be negotiated. Tandemists will be dismayed to learn that Northern Rail (which operates services to both Morecambe and Bridlington) do not currently include tandems in their definition of 'bikes' which can be carried on their trains.

Other options

As long as your bike is in decent condition, there is nothing to stop you from doing the Way of the Roses. There seem to be plenty of electric bikes making the trip across the country, and probably many other weird and wonderful contraptions.

Roses tandemists on the Overton path into York (Day 2)

It is possible, if unadvisable, to do the Way of the Roses on a mountain bike. The resistance caused by wide knobbly tyres would massively increase the amount of effort needed. If you only own a mountain bike, consider investing in some smooth tyres to make your life easier on the tarmac, or hire a bike to do the ride.

Riding solo

Although the most popular option seems to be to ride the Way of the Roses in a group, doing the ride solo allows you to set your own pace and make stops whenever the fancy takes you. Some people are nervous of cycling in packs (maybe those who have grown up watching massive peloton pile-ups in the Tour de France), and others enjoy the freedom of cycling solo. However, cycling solo means you do not gain the slipstream benefits from taking turns at the front and have less support in the case of a breakdown. Make sure you have all the necessary kit and know how to make basic running repairs on your bike if you choose to go it alone.

EQUIPMENT

Carrying your gear

In cycling, travelling light is a top priority. There is a baffling variety of ways to carry your gear, and how much you take and how you carry it depends on several factors: the number of days you are riding, the amount of support you have en route and to what extent you can manage without non-essential extras. It is a matter of personal choice.

Panniers are a long-standing good choice for cycle tourers and

Panniers are a popular choice. Between Wharfe and Stainforth with Pen-y-ghent providing the backdrop (Day 1)

would probably suit those riding the Way of the Roses in four or five days, allowing for carrying picnics and some non-essentials. One obvious downside is that you will need to fit a frame to your bike. There are back- and front-mounted models – a rear-mounted model with two 20-litre bags is most typical. Cyclists wishing to carry oodles of camping equipment might add front panniers. Some people feel that panniers adversely affect the handling of their bike, cause excessive wind resistance and are cumbersome. If your bike already has a pannier rack, but two panniers seem excessive, a happy medium might be a 12-litre trunk bag, which mounts on the top of the rack and doesn't affect the bike's performance as much. If you must, it's possible to cycle with

just one pannier, which should be mounted on the side of the bike away from traffic.

A small daysack with decent chest and waist straps is a simple and cheap option, with a good capacity for cyclists travelling light. Another advantage is that there is no faff when making stops as your valuables are on your back. A daysack also gives cyclists the option of using a hydration bladder. The downside is that – although many groups of Roses riders do use this method – many find a small rucksack uncomfortable, sweaty or unbalancing.

A saddle bag which attaches to the seat and post rather than requiring a rack is another good option for those travelling light, particularly for shorter attempts or where a support vehicle is arriving at the end of the day. Three-litre seat-pack saddle bags are widely and cheaply available, and ideal for those carrying the absolute minimum and making maximum use of the pockets in their cycling jersey. This could be combined with a triangular frame bag which attaches to the bike inside the angle made by the frame to give extra storage.

Saddle packs and larger rigid saddle bags, which use similar attachments but have capacities of up to 17 litres, are becoming more common and are a great option. Some have an extra expandable area ideal for carrying a waterproof and set of evening clothes (although nothing too heavy).

A handlebar bag is an alternative option. These often have a 6- or 7-litre capacity and can include pockets so that your map or bike computer can be viewed while riding. The downsides are that they often sag when heavily loaded and are tricky to fit to some types of bike. A combination of saddle bag/pack and handlebar bag would provide plenty of storage for B&B-ers.

Other equipment

A **basic tool kit** should be the first item on your list. A pump or CO_2 canisters and inflator, spare inner tube or tubes, tyre levers and a set of Allen keys are essential. A puncture repair kit is a back-up for the dreaded double-puncture day. In your group it is useful to have a good bike multi-tool, including screwdrivers, pliers, a knife and spanners. A roll of electrical tape, a few cable ties and a couple of elastic bands can also come in handy.

A **bell** is advisable for warning other path users of your approach on traffic-free sections.

Map, mobile phone, money, credit card and **GPS device** if you use one. Smartphone GPS mapping apps have the drawback of sapping battery power so make sure you have a back-up plan if this is what you are using.

A **bike lock**, though this will depend on how you are riding the route. If you are only stopping at cafés where you can see your bike and overnight accommodation with secure cycle storage (see Appendix A) then you might choose to go without.

Suncream and **very basic toiletries** such as toothbrush and paste, comb and possibly deodorant!

Hydration is crucial so **water bottles** are a must. It is easy to carry two bottles of up to 1-litre capacity in frame cages, but one bottle is fine as the ride never goes a huge distance without passing a shop or other fill-up point.

It is essential to carry some **emergency energy food** even if regular café stops are planned. Never underestimate the impact that a few calories can make on your ability to get up that hill!

Most other gear is a matter of personal choice. For a three-day ride, most people will want to take a change of clothes for the evenings.

Riders passing the remote Keasden church don glasses in bright conditions (Day 1)

WHAT TO WEAR

Helmets

There is no current UK law forcing cyclists to wear helmets and there are still plenty of people who choose not to. Please do not join their ranks and make sure yours is properly fitted and fastened. Helmets are now lightweight and allow airflow to the head.

Clothing

Most people will find that cycling-specific clothing is useful. Depending on temperatures and personal preferences, **cycling shorts or tights** are padded in the right areas and improve comfort during long days in the saddle. These items are designed to be worn without your usual underwear.

Cycling vests usually have several useful features. High-vis colours and reflective strips help make you more eye-catching to other road users, and a dropped back means that there is no draughty gap between top and bottom halves of your clothing. Many cycling jerseys and tops also have large easily accessible back pockets – it's amazing how much gear and food you can cram into these.

A **lightweight waterproof** is also a must. Cycling-specific models include reflectors, pockets and longer backs. They are windproof and are generally designed to pack away compactly.

Wearing **cycling gloves** is again a matter of personal preference and temperature. Some people would not cycle to the corner shop without their gloves, whereas others don't wear them outside of winter. Cycling gloves soak up sweat and allow you to maintain a better grip on the bars. They also include cushioning to lessen the vibration and impact caused by uneven road surfaces. They can also protect the palms in the event of a fall.

In windy or cold weather it can be useful to take an **earband**.

As well as **sunglasses**, many cyclists will wear **clear glasses** in less bright conditions. Others just put up with the odd insect in their eyes and do without. If you are prone to runny eyes when cycling, then glasses are fairly cheap and worth their weight in gold. Contact lens wearers might also find that clear glasses stop their lenses from drying out quickly while riding.

Footwear

The question of footwear might require a little thought. Wear what you are comfortable in. Most relatively firm soled trainers will suffice, and these have the benefits of comfort and saving you carrying extra footwear.

Specific cycling shoes are made with efficient transference of power in mind. The majority now work on a cleat system with clipless pedals and can take a little getting used to. There are several different cleat and pedal systems so you need to make sure yours are compatible; you may need to upgrade your pedals as many lower-priced bikes just come with standard ones. The firm sole of cleated cycling shoes means that little of your effort and power is wasted, but the downside is that they can be uncomfortable to walk in. Interestingly, some studies show that clipless systems actually make many average cyclists less efficient as they encourage upward pulling on the pedals.

Unless you particularly want to waste storage space by taking extra shoes for the evenings, choose footwear that will cover all eventualities (if you are planning to walk around York city centre or up the rough track to Coldstones Cut, for example). Cycling kit companies do seem to have taken note of these problems, with cycling shoes and footwear which looks more like a trainer with flexible or coverable cleat plates becoming more common.

MAPS AND APPS

The maps in this book, along with the detailed route descriptions, should provide everything you need to do the Roses ride and all the day rides described. A Sustrans map of the route is available at the same scale as those in this book. For those who wish to have more detailed mapping, the route is covered at 1:25,000 scale by the following OS sheets: OL41, OL2, 298, 299, 290, 294 and 295. The Ordnance Survey now offers access to all its British maps on computers and mobile devices for a small fee. Other apps such as Viewranger allow users to access parts of OS mapping for a small fee and use Opencyclemap to provide larger scale free maps.

Apps such as Strava have become increasingly popular for logging rides and comparing times and can be very useful for working out an expected average speed and timings. One word of caution: beware of assuming that the distances and particularly cumulative height gains shown on GPS-based apps are exact. During the research for this book the Way of the Roses ride was logged (on one-day, two-day, three-day and five-day itineraries) on apps. The route had been the same but the total ascent data varied wildly from 2272m to 2846m. The actual figure is likely to be somewhere in the middle, around 2500m. The figures at opposite ends of the spectrum were taken from GPS app calculations on a two-day and one-day Roses ride, and my conclusion is that the apps are more accurate for ascent when you ride more slowly. The other warning is that smartphone-based GPS apps tend to deplete batteries, so a bike computer can be a good option.

The route is impressively well signed the whole way across. Some cyclists claim that they have barely needed to consult a map. The route is signed throughout with the small blue pointer signs of the National Cycle Network bearing two small red and white roses. Note that the network numbers of the Roses route change several times during its course, and cyclists should beware following route numbers rather than the rose markers. The Roses route is initially labelled

Roses signage in Clapham (Day 1)

the 69 but soon becomes the 68 at Clapham and subsequently the 688, 67, 65, 658, 66, 164 and finally the 1 on its way into Bridlington. It also shares parts of its distance with long cycle rides such as the Lancashire Cycleway, Yorkshire Dales Cycleway and Yorkshire Wolds Way, so there is often a proliferation of signs.

As of 2017, having checked the route several times, there were signs at all the junctions going west to east (there are marginally fewer on the east-to-west route). Some signs take the form of blue stickers bearing the rose emblems on lampposts and road signposts, and others are easily obscured by foliage. Be eagle-eyed when approaching any junctions and scan the nearby road furniture for the tell-tale rose signs.

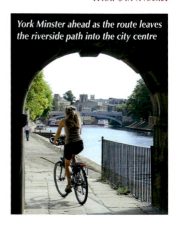

York Minster ahead as the route leaves the riverside path into the city centre

CYCLING DOS AND DON'TS

Some of the Roses route and the day rides are on shared-use traffic-free paths. Be considerate to other users. Slow down – children and dogs often move in unpredictable ways. Ring your bell or call out to pass – no one particularly likes being overtaken by surprise. The most common places to see horse riders is on the Woldgate Roman Road. Always slow down, give horses a wide berth and call out to alert riders if you are passing from behind.

The vast majority of the route is on quiet minor roads. Riding two abreast is legal and more sociable, but do move into single file to let cars past. Make a point of thanking considerate drivers, even those who are merely doing the right thing. It's good karma and it might encourage drivers to continue respecting cyclists.

Scan well ahead of you for hazards; unmarked bends, road furniture, grit and livestock detritus are all common on this route.

Remember to use hand signals at junctions.

WHAT'S IN A NAME?

The Way of the Roses is a neat pun on the Wars of the Roses – a series of medieval battles (1455–87) between the royal houses of Lancaster and York. The romantic-sounding conflict was so called because the emblem of the Lancastrians was a red rose and that of the Yorkists a white one. The rose emblems, as well as adorning the blue cycling signage for this route, will

The county border crossing between Wray and Mewith Head (Day 1)

Homegrown world champion Lizzie Deignan (née Armistead) on her way to winning the 2017 Women's Tour de Yorkshire, on the Roses route at Wilsill (Lizzie is nearest the camera, in orange) (Day 2)

be visible in many 'patriotic' villages along the ride, where county pride and the now friendly rivalry between the two regions are evident. The Wars of the Roses finally ended at the Battle of Bosworth Field in 1485, with the victory of Henry Tudor over Richard III. Shakespeare famously portrayed Richard III as a hunchbacked child-killing villain – he probably did have a major hand in the death of his two young nephews. Whatever his moral failings, he was the last monarch of the House of York. He had strong ties to the city of York and requested to be buried in York Minster (not under a car-park in Leicester as seems to have been the case).

After seeing off Richard III, Henry Tudor became Henry VII and married Elizabeth of York and united the houses of Lancaster and York. Logically England should have ended up with a pink rose emblem, but the Tudors opted for the white-centred red rose heraldic emblem which is used to this day.

None of the major Wars of the Roses battles actually took place near the Roses route, though other bloody battlegrounds such as Stamford Bridge (1066) and Boroughbridge (1322) can be visited along the ride, and the latter did involve a trans-Pennine element. Although the Red Roses came out on top in history, it is the White Rose side which has necessarily won the territorial battle in the Way of the Roses; only 19 miles (30km) of the route are in Lancashire.

CYCLING IN ROSES COUNTRY

Cycling is big news in this neck of the woods. Since the Tour de France visited Yorkshire (and some parts of the Roses route) in 2014, cycling fervour in the White Rose county has reached fever pitch. The Tour de Yorkshire began the following year and appears to be going from strength to strength. In 2017 some Way of the Roses cyclists planned their trip to coincide with watching the Tour de Yorkshire on various parts of their ride. Much of the cycling paraphernalia adorning pubs, village greens and shops along the Roses ride was put in situ when

the Tour de Yorkshire came through town. The ubiquitous sprayed yellow bikes can be seen in numerous villages on the main route and many of the day rides in this book. Added to the effect of the Tours, many smaller villages seem to have a genuine pride in being part of the Way of the Roses route and the floral bikes and so on remain in large part to signal a warm welcome to cyclists and to embrace the economic and cultural benefits that cycling has brought to the region. Finally, although Yorkshire takes the lion's share of the Way of the Roses (and now has its own major annual cycling tour) Lancashire is similarly mad about cycling. The Red Rose county is rife with keen cyclists and hosts many great routes further south of the main Roses ride. Maybe one year the Tour de Yorkshire will reach

An unexpected break en route from Austwick to Settle (Day 2)

Yew Cogar Scar from the steep climb out of Arncliffe (Day ride 3)

out the cycle glove of friendship and take the race across the border!

USING THIS GUIDE

The main Way of the Roses route is described in detail in a three-day itinerary because this seems to be the most common way of tackling the ride. Each day section has a comprehensive route description and detailed maps, as well as smaller scale ones where the route goes through populated areas. Points at which it is important to pay attention to the navigation are highlighted, as well as potentially hazardous road crossings and descents. Also included in each day section is a route profile, showing where the main climbs and descents take place.

For each section you will find a route information box. This details key information you need to know before going on the ride such as mileage, ascent and refreshment stops. Total ascents are approximate and the gradients mentioned refer to the steepest parts of the climbs. The route information is followed by a brief summary of the key features of the day's riding ahead, followed by detailed directions. Details of worthwhile variations are given at the appropriate points within the main route description. Cycling times are not given in the route information boxes as these vary wildly depending on fitness, load, weather and terrain. Broadly speaking an average party could aim to cover between 8–12 miles per hour, not including stops.

Itineraries for cyclists planning to ride the Way of the Roses in two-, four- or five-day sections are given in the Route Summary Tables. Details of distances, ascents, stops and refreshments are included, but cyclists should refer to the three-day itinerary for the detailed description of the route.

The day rides

These additional rides are all located around the corridor taken by the Way of the Roses. In some cases they cross or link to the main route, but none start more than a few miles from the Way. The day rides have been designed to follow the premise of the main Roses route as closely as possible, while showcasing some of the areas that the main route cannot possibly visit on its way across the country. Each route is a circular day ride of substantial length (with the exception of Route 6 which is linear). The premise is that a cyclist aiming to complete the Roses three-day ride would find these routes of a similar difficulty to a day of the Way.

The day rides, like the Way of the Roses, use mainly minor roads and bits of cycle paths where possible. They are all passable on a sturdy road bike. They link spectacular scenery and places of interest, so offer cyclists different perspectives on the landscapes of Lancashire and Yorkshire.

GPX tracks

GPX tracks for the routes in this guidebook are available to download free at www.cicerone.co.uk/912/GPX. A GPS device is an excellent aid to navigation, but you should also carry a map and compass and know how to use them.

Enterprising sales tactics on the Way of the Roses after Stamford Bridge (Day 3)

THE WAY OF THE ROSES

Taking a sharp corner where the Roses route shares the road with the Yorkshire Wolds Way near Millington (Day 3)

THE THREE-DAY RIDE

DAY 1
Morecambe to Burnsall

Start	Morecambe – The Bastion, Main Promenade SD 427 643
Finish	Burnsall SE 032 613
Distance	53 miles (85km)
Total ascent	980m
Steepest climb	High Hill Lane, Settle – officially 20% (though many cyclists believe it peaks at closer to 30%!)
Terrain	Surfaced cycle path to Crook o'Lune, minor roads to Settle, with three short sections on B roads and one brief section on a gravel cycle path avoiding the busy A65
OS maps	OL41 Forest of Bowland & Ribblesdale, OL2 Yorkshire Dales – Southern & Western Area
Refreshments	Morecambe, Lancaster, Crook o'Lune, Hornby, Wray, Clapham, Austwick, Settle, Airton, Hetton, Cracoe, Burnsall
Intermediate distances	Lancaster 4 miles (6km), Hornby 15 miles (24km), Clapham 25 miles (40km), Settle 35 miles (56km), Cracoe 48 miles (77km)

A great day's cycling lies ahead – the charms of the route quickly win you over and continue to impress as the miles clock up. From the frequently windblown promenade in Morecambe, stretch your legs by cycling along the seafront to pay tribute to comedy legend Eric Morecambe at his nearby statue. The day starts in a leisurely fashion on the link route to Lancaster and onwards via a disused railway line to the Crook o' Lune without any traffic or ascent. Here the route takes on a different guise as you climb through the beautiful Forest of Bowland and use peaceful lanes along the side of the Lune Valley. Descend through the pretty Red Rose villages of Gressingham, Hornby and Wray, before leaving the Lune and gaining height to enter Yorkshire. The White Rose county is heralded by the impressive sight of 723m Ingleborough, one of the famous Three Peaks. From here, the undulating road to Clapham is idyllic and gives surprisingly simple cycling.

It is obligatory to stop off in the bustling small market town of Settle to sample one of the many teashops while contemplating the day's next objective. The climb out of Settle is the steepest of the whole route. It's undoubtedly the toughest test of the day (and indeed of the whole Way of the Roses), but those who huff and puff up the twisty hill will have their efforts rewarded as a marvellous limestone landscape opens up and the ancient geology of the Yorkshire Dales is revealed.

The climb is followed by a superb descent into Airton and continues across undulating terrain through the lovely Dales villages of Winterburn and Hetton to Cracoe. The day finishes with a flourish on a climb over to Wharfedale via a beautiful narrow lane to reach the quintessential Dales village of Burnsall.

The large Way of the Roses sign on the promenade at **Morecambe** is the official start of the route. Some cyclists will no doubt want to go down the nearby ramp to the beach to dip a toe into the Irish Sea (this can be a surprisingly long walk if the tide is out). It is definitely a good

Roses riders stretching their legs on Morecambe's promenade

MORECAMBE AND MORECAMBE BAY

The Art Deco Midland Hotel from the Stone Jetty

The statue of Eric Morecambe was designed by Graham Ibbeson and was unveiled in 1999 by HM The Queen. Pub quiz aficionados will know that Eric was born John Eric Bartholomew but subsequently took the name of his beloved hometown. The words of the Morecambe and Wise theme tune 'Bring Me Sunshine' are engraved on the steps leading up to the statue. Maybe singing a rousing verse or two will help the weather treat you kindly on your forthcoming ride.

The Stone Jetty is all that now remains of what was once Morecambe harbour. It was rebuilt in 1995 as part of ongoing coastal defence work. It is a good place for a gentle warm-up pedal to view the sculpted seabirds of the Tern Project (see below) and the town's much-vaunted art deco hotel.

Bring me sunshine... the Eric Morecambe statue on Morecambe seafront

There are two distinct kinds of seagull in Morecambe: firstly the swooping, squawking, sandwich-stealing kind and secondly the flocks of metal ones. Thankfully the latter are not flying round and dive-bombing your fish and chips, but have been created as part of a large art installation called the Tern Project. As a result, cormorants, gulls and gannets of the steel variety line the railings and fences around the seafront and rusty razorbills perch on the town's several roundabouts.

The mudflats of Morecambe Bay are infamous for both their quicksand and even quicker moving tides. It is possible to walk right across the bay in the company of expert local guides. The bay's notoriety grew after 2004's cockling disaster, in which 23 mistreated and illegal Chinese cockle pickers were tragically drowned here when they were caught by the incoming tide.

idea, before heading inland, to ride up and down a few hundred metres of the refurbished promenade. This gives you the chance to warm up your muscles, double check your bike is in the best working order and perhaps rendezvous with your Way of the Roses cycling companions. As you stretch your legs and breathe in the bracing sea air, make sure to look out across the notoriously treacherous mud flats of Morecambe Bay. Just a stone's throw from the start of the route is the statue of the town's most famous son, comedian Eric Morecambe. Also on the promenade are the art deco Midland Hotel and some public artworks, the first a metal profile of the many (sometimes visible) Lakeland mountains. Right at the start

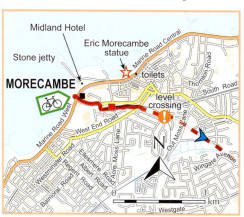

of the ride, it is worth riding out to sea along the Stone Jetty to view its numerous gull-themed sculptures. The nearest public toilets are 500 metres northwards along the promenade.

Take the road directly opposite the Way of the Roses start placard, heading inland across the small roundabout. Pass a bowling alley and continue to a larger roundabout adorned by more metal seabirds. Here the route signage, somewhat confusingly, aims to shepherd cyclists across a zebra crossing and onto the pavement on the right-hand side of the roundabout (if you end up at Morecambe train station you have gone too far). The route takes the exit which appears to lead into a restaurant car-park. Thankfully this is not the case and instead a tarmac bridleway materialises on your left. This is the welcome start of the long traffic-free initial section of the route which spans the urban area between Morecambe and Lancaster. The bridleway cuts down the side of the railway and shortly crosses a southern branch line at a gated level crossing. ◀

There is no barrier and cyclists should stop and have their wits about them.

The bridleway is designed so that cyclists use one side and pedestrians the other, and is clearly signed. It is a well-travelled path so keep an eye out for other users. The path becomes more pleasant as the outskirts of Morecambe are left behind and you emerge alongside the River Lune in Lancashire's historic county town of **Lancaster**. This stretch is known as St George's Quay and the river here is tidal and edged by salt marsh. Lancaster's castle can be seen from here and the dome of the Ashton Memorial is also visible high above the town. Turn right over the arcing Lune suspension bridge towards the town centre, then go left and ride up the opposite bank of the river. After the suspension bridge a short detour turning right following cycling signs for 400 metres can be made to see the castle or to visit Lancaster's town centre.

Lancaster's castle is a medieval fortress which served as a prison from 1196 to 2011. During that time, it saw more hangings than anywhere else in the UK outside of London. Nowadays you don't have to be a wrongdoer to pay a visit as it has become a museum.

In the 18th century, shipbuilding was a major part of Lancaster's economy. It took place

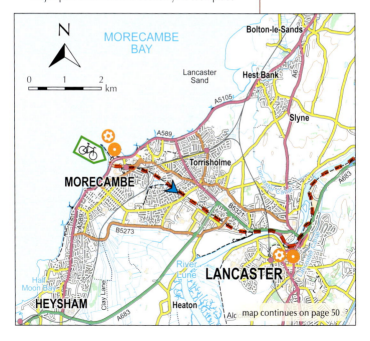

map continues on page 50

Making an escape – the former prison at Lancaster Castle

on the north side of the river by the present-day Millennium Bridge, and the Port of Lancaster was a busy place. In the early 19th century, trade declined and Lancaster looked to other industries to revive its fortunes. Lancaster's Maritime Museum, based in the nearby Custom House, has more information about the city's shipping heritage.

The route bends with the river; look out for a sharp right turn leading through an underpass to emerge at a small riverside park, still following the course of the Lune. The amenable cycle path becomes the Lune Riverside Walk and is well used – expect to share this section with hikers and dog walkers. Ride through a small tunnel under the Lune Aqueduct.

The **Lune Aqueduct** carries the Lancaster canal over the River Lune. It was designed by John Rennie, whose other works include four of London's famous bridges: Waterloo, Southwark, the old Vauxhall Bridge and London Bridge itself.

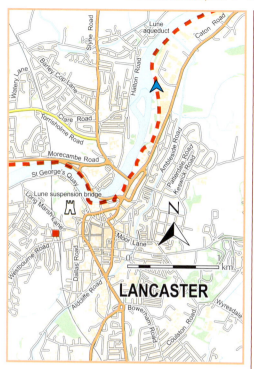

Passing the Lune Aqueduct on the riverside path

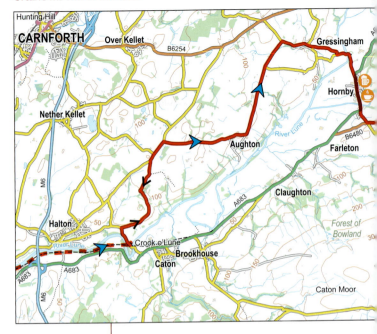

Continue amid pleasant wooded scenery. The route then takes the abandoned railway line under the M6 (though you'll scarcely notice) past the former Halton station and eventually across one half of the Lune Viaduct.

The disused Skipton–Morecambe railway line was known as the **Little North Western Railway**. The section crossing the two Crook o' Lune viaducts opened in 1849 and was run by the Midland Railway until it was condemned to closure for passengers by the Beeching Report of 1966. The striking double viaduct has thankfully now had a new lease of life as a footpath and cycleway.

Here a large kiosk sells hot drinks and the usual egg and bacon sandwiches and might be welcomed by cyclists who had an early start.

The route forks left shortly afterwards up a little rise to the **Crook o' Lune** viewpoint. ◀

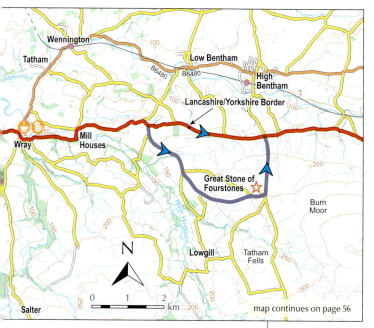

The **Crook o' Lune** is the romantic name of a sharp bend in the River Lune where the rise of the land allows superb views across the open valley. A painting by J M W Turner in 1816 immortalised the scenery at the Crook o' Lune. The original artwork can be seen in London's Courtauld Gallery.

Leave the Crook o' Lune car-park and turn right onto a surprisingly busy road for 400 metres until forking off right uphill on a quiet surfaced lane over a cattle grid. The rest of the Lancashire section of the route goes through the Forest of Bowland Area of Outstanding Natural Beauty. As you embark upon the first climb of the day, the spectacular nature of the Way of the Roses reveals itself as the views expand over the Lune Valley. The climb is steeper than might be expected and the route takes a

The pastoral view at the Crook o' Lune, painted by J M W Turner

Gourmets might associate the name of the village with Gressingham duck meat. Although the duck – a cross between a mallard and a Pekin – did originate in the village, it is now exclusively bred and farmed in East Anglia.

right near the top. Just as cyclists will be relishing their first downhill of the day, there is another right turn sign-posted to **Aughton**, which is easy to miss. This minor road undulates through lovely pastoral scenery for 3 miles (5km) until it takes a right onto a wider road to the pretty village of **Gressingham**, with its 12th-century church. It is well worth pausing here for a swig of water. ◀

It will soon become obvious that the **Forest of Bowland** is not actually a forest. The name comes from the medieval definition of the word: an area reserved by the king for hunting. The Forest of Bowland is an upland of gritstone fells and peat moorland surrounded by the lush Ribble, Hodder, Lune and Wyre valleys. It covers a 202sq km section of Lancashire and North Yorkshire.

Go straight through Gressingham and soon cross the Lune on a picturesque bridge and continue into **Hornby**, filtering right onto the main road through the village where there are two pubs and a great little tearoom (as well as a privately owned castle). The River Lune is left behind here but the straightforward and enjoyable riding continues. Where Hornby's main street bends, take a left (straight ahead) and then turn left again to reach the pretty village of **Wray**, where there is a post office, pub and the Greenfoot Farm café. Turn right in Wray and, after a mile, start to gain height, with the expansive vista of the Three Peaks area of the Yorkshire Dales opening up before you. The peak of Ingleborough is most prominent in the view to your left.

The hen harrier – emblem of the Forest of Bowland at Hornby

Whernside (736m), Ingleborough (723m) and Pen-y-ghent (694m) were arguably the original Three Peaks. As it became increasingly popular to invent challenges involving the British peaks of Ben Nevis, Snowdon and Scafell Pike, the 'Yorkshire' epithet was added to distinguish the two summit trios. As a result, the mountains are now most commonly known outside the local area as **'The Yorkshire 3 Peaks'**.

Crossing the Lune bridge between Gressingham and Hornby

Take a right at a stone bus shelter towards Lowgill and 150 metres later a left signposted to Settle (12 miles/19km) along a superb minor road where views of Ingleborough dominate. The route shortly crosses the border from Lancashire into North Yorkshire and this momentous change is heralded by a road sign.

Great Stone of Fourstones Detour

For those keen to mark their passage from Lancashire into Yorkshire in a more memorable fashion, this is a well worthwhile short detour (adding less than 2 miles to the main route) with a little extra height gain to see a massive glacial erratic which historically marked the county border. By climbing the 15 carved steps to the top of the stone you gain superb views of the impressive trio of Yorkshire's Three Peaks.

The Great Stone of Fourstones, marking the Lancashire/ Yorkshire border

The **Great Stone** is situated just 10 metres from the modern county border (actually on the Yorkshire side). Legend has it that the devil himself dropped the huge stone on his way north to make the Devil's Bridge at Kirkby Lonsdale. Another tale is that it was

hurled in anger across the Irish Sea by the giant Finn McCool, whose other works include The Giant's Causeway in Northern Ireland. It is believed, as the name suggests, that there were once four stones in a natural circle. The others may have been broken up and used to make tools or buildings.

To visit the stone, turn right at the stone bus shelter on the main route, but continue straight ahead instead of turning left to Settle. This is marked as the 90 cycle route to Lowgill and Slaidburn. Continue, climbing gently for less than a mile, then take a left, still on the 90 towards Slaidburn. After another mile turn left at a T-junction in open moorland. This is signed to Bentham and the 90 is left behind here. The stone becomes apparent to your left – there is a path to it about 100 metres after the junction. After your visit carry on down the same road for nearly a mile to re-join the main Roses route by turning right (to Settle) at a crossroads with a small petrol station.

Main route continues

Keep straight ahead (to Settle) at a small crossroads where there is a petrol station with a basic shop. ▶ Continue ascending to **Mewith Head** where the road goes through beautiful moorland to the hamlet of **Keasden** and its remote church; 100 metres later turn left and descend steeply to a lovely stone humpback bridge. Climb slightly under the arches of the railway line and then enjoy the easy cycling to **Clapham**.

Just before Clapham village, the route crosses the busy A65. Take care here or use the signed underpass to get across into the village centre.

In **Clapham** there is a visitor centre, café, pub, post office and cave rescue centre. This area of the Yorkshire Dales provides some of the best caving in the country.

Turn right just after the bridge in Clapham towards Settle. After a mile, this brings you out leftwards onto a

Take care on the sporadic descents on this road which can be covered with farm dirt and grit on the bendy dips, requiring a cautious approach.

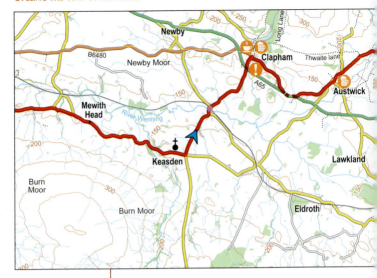

crafty section of segregated gritty cycle path which runs alongside the A65 for 400 metres before shepherding you leftwards onto the minor road to Austwick. It is on this section that the route enters the Yorkshire Dales National Park. As the road winds into **Austwick**, the hillsides bear the scars of the limestone outcrops that form the bedrock of this part of the county.

> The story of the **Yorkshire Dales** began 350 million years ago, when the Dales would have been a warm shallow sea with coral reefs. Fossilised sea creatures produced the beautiful limestone, and coarse windblown sand formed a layer of gritstone on top. The dales (valleys) were then carved out by Ice Age glaciers.

> The undulating road from Austwick to Settle continues to delight. After 4 miles (6.5km) the route turns off right gently uphill onto an even quieter road, passing the limestone-topped hump of Smearsett Scar to your right.

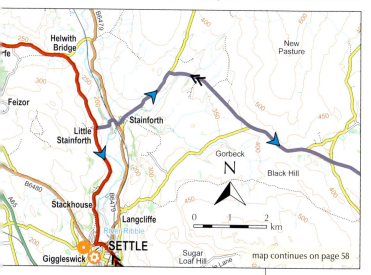

map continues on page 58

After **Little Stainforth** the descent to Settle is gradual and relaxing, with the strange quarried hillside and Stainforth Scar to the left.

The Malham Tarn Detour

This superb alternative route leaves the main Roses itinerary at Little Stainforth, 2 miles before Settle, and re-joins it at Airton. It follows part of the Yorkshire Dales Cycleway, which is signed with a Swaledale sheep's head logo. As well as being a superb alternative in its own right, the detour offers the opportunity to visit the jaw-dropping Malham Cove and avoid the testing High Hill Lane climb out of Settle. ▶

Leave the main Roses route at Little Stainforth, turning left signed as the Malham Tarn detour. After 200 metres cross the River Ribble on a narrow stone bridge and then climb to cross the B6479, turning right then left 50 metres later into **Stainforth** village (toilets). Here turn left and tackle the stiff climb out of the village. After 1½ miles take a right turn down a cruel dip and steeply up

This route does not have consistent signage so a little care is needed.

57

again to reach the huge limestone plateau which houses the high glacial tarn. Continue with superb views of Pen-y-ghent to your left then merge left at a junction after nearly 3 miles (5km).

After another mile take a right fork signed only to High Trenhouse, crossing a cattle grid after 20 metres. In 700 metres the main route into Malham turns right at a crossroads, but continue straight ahead to skirt the southern side of the visible Malham Tarn, passing a small chimney to your right. The road eventually curves right at a wooden signpost and begins a long descent. Here there are good examples

Passing Pen-y-ghent high on the Malham Tarn plateau

of the clints and grykes of natural limestone paving, the most stunning example of which can be found at the top of Malham Cove. Turn right at the T-junction after a

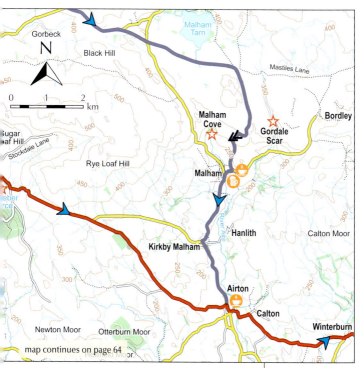

map continues on page 64

long steep downhill to enter the pretty village of **Malham** (another good choice for refreshments should they be needed). The route heads out left after crossing the river. The breathtaking limestone edifice of Malham Cove can be visited on foot by turning right here and following signs for about 20 minutes.

Malham Cove is a natural wonder – an 80m-high sheer curving cliff formed by a waterfall of glacial meltwater after the last Ice Age. Sport climbers can often be seen swinging from the bolts that someone has seen fit to drill into this immense piece of rock.

The short walk to visit Malham Cove is well worth the effort

Head out of Malham (following signs to Airton), climbing slightly, with views of the cove behind you. Continue through Kirby Malham on to **Airton**. Here the route re-joins the Way of the Roses (straight ahead).

Main route continues

At the end of the road turn left into the small market town of **Settle**.

Around the bustling market place there are numerous shops, cafés and pubs vying for your custom and **Settle** seems a sensible choice for a pitstop to recharge the batteries, as the toughest climb of the whole route is tackled next. The Singing Kettle on the main street is unbeatable value, whereas many cyclists seem to be tempted by the unusually named Ye Olde Naked Man café a few doors away. Whatever refreshments are taken on board, be careful not to overdo it on the cake as you'll pay for it on the hills ahead.

The market town of Settle is a popular stop for cyclists

Follow signs behind the large building in the market place to take a road aptly named High Hill Lane. This quickly steepens over a short initial cobbled section and then climbs out of the village through a few bends with an exceptionally evil gradient. This steep section goes on further than you might think, so pace yourself accordingly and watch out for descending vehicles particularly if you're using the full width of the road in a bid to stay on your bike (don't worry if you end up pushing – you won't be the first and you certainly won't be the last cyclist to be defeated here).

Eventually there is some brief respite and a chance to rest the legs before a final kick up to the summit. On the way views of Pendle Hill (back in Lancashire), over to the right, provide a brief distraction. Console yourself in the knowledge that there is nothing else this tough on the remainder of the route. It might sound like hell, but the pain is more than made up for by the stunning scenery – and the chance to climb into a dramatic landscape with only a few sheep for company.

Scaleber Force is easily accessed from a dip with a signpost near the final climb of High Hill Lane.

Taking on the Roses ride in winter might be a much tougher undertaking – near Scaleber Force, high above Settle

The otherworldly clints and grykes on top of Malham Cove

The 12m fall cascades over limestone into a small plunge pool just below the road. It might be a good place to stop and let tired party members catch up.

The climb eventually ends at a cattle grid – sit back and relax, or at least assume a comfy position for the long descent into Airton. This should be relatively trouble-free, but near the steepest section care is needed at a cattle grid on a bend. Further caution is advised close to the bottom of the descent where the road surface deteriorates slightly through tree cover. Turn right at the village of **Airton**, then quickly left over the River Aire (after which the village is rather obviously named). ◄ Make a short climb up to **Calton**, followed by a short descent to cross a bridge at **Winterburn** and a final pull over to **Hetton** (with its famous gastropub, the Angel Inn). Here the ridge of fells on Embsay Moor can be seen more clearly and the rock has changed from the limestone of the Settle area into Yorkshire gritstone country. The crags of Rylstone, Rolling Gate and Crookrise are all visible, along with the Cracoe war memorial tower on the end of the ridge.

There is a very good spacious café in Airton, just a few hundred metres off route towards Malham.

The distinctive white limestone which is predominant around Clapham and Settle in the western dales stands atop a dripping network of **caves and sinkholes** which permeate the hills nearby. East of Airton gritstone becomes predominant and the heathery moors are crowned with its generally smaller and darker buttresses.

Rise slightly out of Hetton to cross a barriered level crossing and continue to join the busy B6265 going left through **Cracoe**. About 300 metres past Cracoe there is a sharp bend in the busy road. Here the route turns off right and much care must be taken at the awkward junction.

Once on the minor single-track road to Thorpe it is simple cycling once again as you climb gently between snaking dry-stone walls and fantastic Dales landscapes. The road surface is somewhat gritty so take care as the lane drops to a dip. The route is technical enough to put the onus on safety rather than speed, and this allows time to take in the wonderful surroundings. The lane goes right to join a slightly more well-used thoroughfare at the hamlet of **Thorpe**. After this the craggy-topped fell of

Cyclists enjoying the scenic stretch of narrow walled road between Cracoe and Burnsall

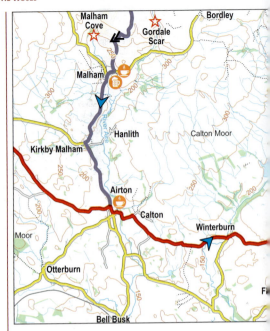

Simon's Seat is a feature of the view ahead. Take care on the descent here, as the sharp bends are unmarked and the dry-stone walls are not forgiving to cyclists who get it wrong. Turn right at a T-junction to continue the descent into the picture-postcard village of **Burnsall** and a satisfying end to the first stage of the route.

The **lovely village of Burnsall** with its five-arched bridge has long been a popular spot for day-trippers who come to paddle in the river, walk along the banks of the Wharfe and take advantage of the tearooms in the village which are frequented by Yorkshire's Olympic triathlon heroes Alistair and Johnny Brownlee. There are also two pubs with accommodation and food, a few B&Bs, and the village hall also serves as a bunkhouse.

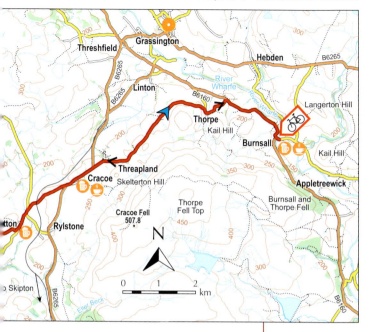

There is camping a mile further along the route at Appletreewick, where you can stay in an on-site VW campervan or a yurt, as well as pitch your own tent.

EAST TO WEST

This section of the route is arguably even more rewarding in this direction. The hills are tackled early on and the climb from Airton to Settle is much less punishing than its opposite number. There are very few opportunities for going wrong, and this is also the shortest day section of the ride.

Take care on the extremely steep and winding descent into Settle down High Hill Lane. Test your brakes before descending.

Make sure you take the road to Hornby out of Wray (the signs are not obvious).

DAY 2
Burnsall to York

Start	Burnsall SE 032 613
Finish	York city centre SE 602 523
Distance	58 miles (93km)
Total ascent	1005m
Steepest climb	New Road, Appletreewick 14%
Terrain	Mainly quiet minor roads (some of which have a less-than-perfect surface). One 8-mile (13km) stretch on the busier B6265 around Pateley Bridge and a shorter stretch on the same road into Ripon. A short well-surfaced traffic-free section through Studley Park and a longer and slower riverside path into York.
OS maps	Explorers 298 Nidderdale, 299 Ripon & Boroughbridge, 290 York
Refreshments	Appletreewick, Stump Cross Caverns, Toft Gate, Pateley Bridge, Glasshouses, Brimham Rocks, Fountains Abbey, Ripon, Bishop Monkton, Boroughbridge, Aldborough, Lower Dunsforth, Great Ouseburn, Linton-on-Ouse, Beningbrough Hall, York
Intermediate distances	Pateley Bridge 10 miles (16km), Fountains Abbey 21 miles (34km), Ripon 26 miles (42km), Boroughbridge 35 miles (56km), Great Ouseburn 42 miles (68km), Beningbrough Hall 48 miles (77km)

The second day is almost a reversal of its predecessor. Whereas Day 1 began steadily on easy flat paths, Day 2 shows its hand more immediately with a majestic climb out of Wharfedale and exhilarating lofty views right from the start. There are so many excellent diversions calling for your attention on the first half of the day's ride that it is difficult to stay in the saddle, let alone make haste on the nearly 60 miles (97km) that beckon towards the day's final destination of York. With chocolate-box villages like Appletreewick and Pateley Bridge, natural showcaves, one of England's largest pieces of public art, otherworldly rock formations at Brimham and the spectacular Fountains Abbey all on route, it seems a shame not to linger longer. The historic tiny city of Ripon marks the halfway point of today's ride, but cyclists will no doubt spend far more time in the hilly terrain of the first half of the route.

By contrast, the 30 miles (48km) from Ripon to York will pass much more quickly and the senses get a chance to take a break and let the legs power into the more gentle territory of the Vale of York and its immaculate villages. The final stretch to York provides a fitting climax as the route takes off-road options to emerge unexpectedly on the Ouse waterfront in the city centre and swoops through the ancient city walls to finish at the towering grandeur of York Minster. It is an unforgettable end to a magnificent day's cycling.

In **Burnsall** cross the humped stone bridge over the River Wharfe. The route crosses the long-distance Dales Way footpath here, which takes hikers north to Kendal. The day begins with pleasantly undulating cycling to **Appletreewick**, another popular Dales village.

The twee-sounding name conjures up images of times gone by and is sometimes shortened to **Aptrick** by locals. The village gives access to a

Climbing up from Appletreewick, with the crags of Simon's Seat beyond

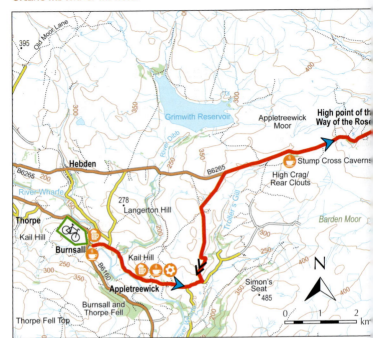

lovely stretch of the River Wharfe and the spot has
a hugely popular campsite at which passing cyclists

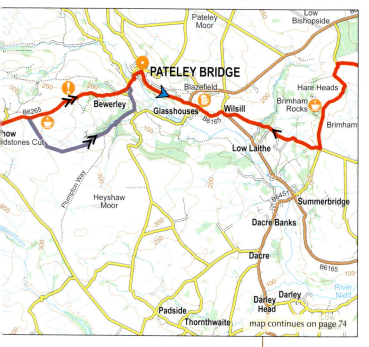

map continues on page 74

can get a tea or coffee, as well as two pubs (the New Inn has a bike livery behind it).

At the end of the village lies the first big challenge of the day: a stiff climb up and out of Wharfedale to reach the highest point on the Way of the Roses at 404m near Greenhow. The road splits and the route goes leftwards uphill, with the initial bend being the steepest part of this passage. Unlike the hill out of Settle, the Appletreewick climb has restful stretches where the views right to the gritstone-topped fell of Simon's Seat and later the trough of Troller's Gill will more than compensate for any aching leg muscles. This is my favourite climb of the route – it is interesting and tough enough to be satisfying without being too sustained.

69

GREENHOW

Rudyard Kipling wrote a short story about Greenhow which stated: 'You could tell Greenhow Hill folk from the red colour of their cheeks and nose tips and their blue eyes driven into pin points by the wind.' Whether or not this is an accurate depiction of Greenhow's modern residents, you are certain to feel the chill wind here and want to zip up warmly on all but the hottest summer day.

One of the Mouseman's weathered mice at Greenhow, with Coldstones Cut beyond

It is worth pausing for a moment at the cemetery's wooden lych gate, which was carved by Robert Thompson (1876–1955) – better known as The Mouseman. Some of his tell-tale mice are snugly hidden away in the eaves of the gateway. More Mouseman mice can be found in Bridlington Priory at the end of the Roses route.

Lead mining took place in Greenhow as far back as Roman times. In the 14th century, Greenhow lead was used to build the roof of Windsor Castle. The area was a hive of industry and once boasted three pubs, with lime burning, lead mining and stone quarrying providing work. The huge Coldstones Quarry functions to this day a mile or so further along the route. The miners built St Mary's Church in the village using local stone, and it remains to this day the highest church in England (427m above sea level).

The Way continues to rise gently to meet the B6265 road to Pateley Bridge. This is the busiest and fastest stretch of tarmac on which the route spends any significant time (6 miles/10km into Pateley Bridge then another 1½ miles to Wilsill). It is hugely exposed to the elements and there are often strong crosswinds here. There is no reasonable alternative so take care turning right onto the wide road and enjoy flatter terrain until a further short rise brings you to **Stump Cross Caverns**, a natural Victorian showcave (great café). If you choose to stop here, just before the highest point of the route, take care turning off right into the caverns' car-park. ▶

The route climbs just a little more before reaching the settlement of **Greenhow** and the high point of the Way just before the village. Shortly after Stump Cross Caverns, the route enters the Nidderdale Area of Outstanding Natural Beauty (bafflingly not part of the national park). If you approach Greenhow on a sunny day, the russet and amber tones of the moorland mix with dappled patches of green and yellow stretching out for miles. Conversely, in all but perfect weather, the area can seem bleak and the views often non-existent. Pass a lonely playground, a water tower, a war memorial and a graveyard.

About a mile after Greenhow, pass the entrance to Coldstones Quarry and shortly afterwards a car-park for Coldstones Cut.

These limestone showcaves have a spooky selection of stalagmites and stalagtites. Prehistoric bones of reindeer and wolverines were discovered in the cave in the 1920s.

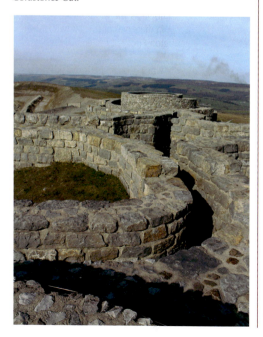

The labyrinthine stonework at Coldstones Cut

Coldstones Cut is a double spiral of hilltop walkways built out of stone from the huge working quarry it overlooks. Depending on who's measuring it, it is Yorkshire or the UK's biggest public artwork and it's about a 15-minute walk uphill from the Roses route (hybrid riders may wish to cycle up).

Toft Gate Lime Kiln is very close to the site of the Coldstones Cut. The flues, chimney and kiln at the site are remarkably intact. Lime was produced here for five decades and even local children used to do the dangerous work here, breaking down limestone in the sweltering heat to make quick lime for mortar and fertiliser.

This technical descent has been the scene of several accidents and there is an alternative via a right turn just before Coldstones which leads down a minor road (just as steeply) into Pateley via Bewerley.

As you begin the descent into Pateley Bridge, savour the expansive views across Nidderdale and beyond to the Vale of York, where the route heads later in the day. There are numerous signs warning cyclists and motorists about the hazards of the way ahead; ignore them at your peril. ◄

Breathe a sigh of relief as you enter the village of **Pateley Bridge** past the park and over the River Nidd into town.

A right turn straight after the bridge takes you along Nidd Walk for 200 metres to the **Pillars Past sculpture**, which is part of a proposed series of artworks to be installed along the Way of the Roses route. The sculpture celebrates various facets of Nidderdale life and depicts a monk from Fountains Abbey, a sheep farmer and a miner.

The Pillars Past sculpture at Pateley Bridge was specially commissioned for the Way of the Roses

Pateley Bridge is a treasure trove of great independent shops and cafés. Its steep old high street boasts a quality butcher, bakery, sweet shop, pancake house and various cafés – there is so much to tempt a weary biker that it is well-nigh impossible to contemplate the final major climb up to Brimham Rocks without partaking of some of these

Crossing Pateley Bridge

multitudinous refreshments. Talbot House tearooms on the main street has sumptuous cake and scones.

Head up the steep and narrow high street and follow the road as it bends rightwards at the top of the village, passing a chapel and the site of the former Nidderdale Brewery. The fairly busy road climbs steadily. Ignore a first turning to Brimham and continue past the **Glasshouses** crossroads, descending slightly to **Wilsill**. Here the route leaves the B6265 and takes a minor road up left. This dips down through Smelthouses and climbs again steeply towards Brimham Rocks. At the hilltop, turn left onto Brimham Moor Road. The incongruous massive golf balls of Menwith Hill come into view. The first buttress of Brimham is straight ahead and the main entrance 500 metres further along on the left.

The giant golf balls at RAF Menwith Hill make up the biggest **communications monitoring station** in the world, providing intelligence to both the UK and USA. The facility is operated by the top-secret

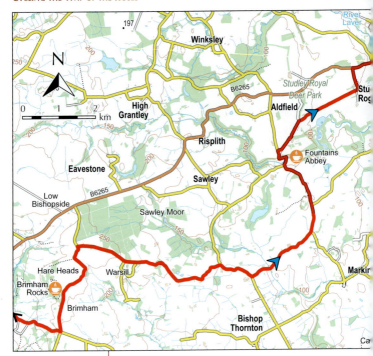

The rocks at Brimham have longstanding individual names and, with a little imagination, it is usually possible to spot the likenesses. The most bizarre are the Dancing Bear, the Sphinx, the Idol and Lover's Leap.

American National Security Agency (NSA) and detractors question the ethics of hosting this 'spy base' in the beautiful Yorkshire countryside. The golf balls have now multiplied from the initial four in the 1970s to more than 30.

Brimham Rocks is the ideal place to stop if you have bought a picnic in Pateley, as it marks the end of the real climbing for the day (and indeed the whole route). The surreal gritstone towers are on National Trust land and are popular with climbers, scramblers, ramblers and adventurous children alike. The site is free to enter and has a visitor centre (refreshment kiosk selling ice cream and hot drinks). ◄

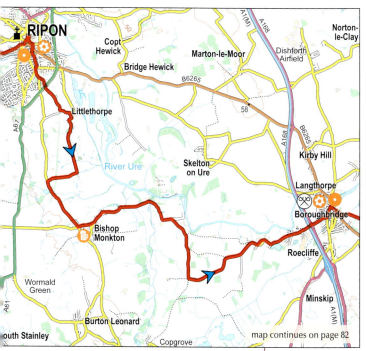

map continues on page 82

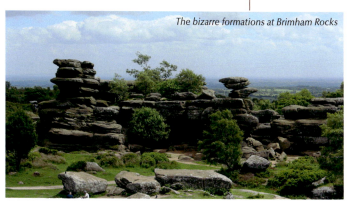

The bizarre formations at Brimham Rocks

Brimham Moor is most beautiful in summer when it blooms with the deep purple of heather and the lush green fronds of bracken. Skirt round the Brimham Rocks site, with several of the mushroom formations visible from the road. After leaving the rocks behind, take a small right turn signposted to Brimham Rocks Cottages that is easy to miss. The flat and expansive Vale of York seems to stretch out ahead, but we have a little way to go before crossing it. Continue through attractive woodland, beginning a long and extremely gradual descent to less lofty territory. There are still a few surprises left in store today though.

After 3 miles (5km) turn right at the first T-junction and then 500 metres later take a left down an unmarked road that has a less-than-perfect surface. As you come over the brow of the hill, a view of the gatehouse of **Fountains Abbey** appears. Unfortunately, the beautiful and renowned Cistercian abbey itself cannot be clearly seen from the route so now is the time to decide whether to make time to visit this spectacular site (fee charged, NT members free). Descend to a dip at a back entrance to the abbey grounds. Even if you are planning to visit

The resplendent ruins of Fountains Abbey

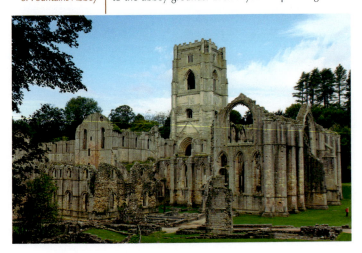

The beeline view to distant Ripon Cathedral from Studley Royal

the abbey, press on past this entrance and after a short rise, take a right turn up the drive at the abbey's main entrance. Bikes are not allowed into the abbey (café) so if you want to stop here, leave your bike in a rack by the visitor centre. If time is short, head straight across a small roundabout at the visitor centre and look out for a large obelisk where a delightful section of the route takes a little gate to enter the grounds of Studley Royal Deer Park on a lane owned by the National Trust. ▸

Studley Royal Deer Park is home to around 500 wild red, fallow and sika deer. There is a very good chance of seeing them, particularly at quieter times of the day.

Fountains Abbey is suitably impressive as its status as the UK's largest monastic ruin – once home to more than 1000 monks – would suggest. It suffered the same fate as most of its contemporaries, at the hands of serial groom Henry VIII.

The striking church of St Mary was built in 1870 by the Marquis and Marchioness of Ripon. It was aligned and raised up perfectly to look out along the long straight road which commands a direct view of the distant Ripon Cathedral. If you have time, have a look inside at its exquisite stained glass windows, floor mosaics and strange animal carvings.

As you swoop through the park keep your eyes peeled for deer. Ride over triple cattle grids as you exit the estate and a single one a little further along. At this point it feels as if you could cycle on full steam ahead right to the door of Ripon Cathedral, but the way ahead is barred, so the road swings left.

Turn right onto the B6265 to **Ripon**. Engage top gear and cruise easily into town. The route into the city centre is well marked. It involves turning right at a small roundabout and then left at some traffic lights and then right to enter the main square where there are public toilets and numerous shops and cafés.

The **Ripon Hornblower** sets the watch for the city by sounding the horn at 9pm every evening in the main square. This ritual has happened every single night for 1100 years, since Alfred the Great originally bestowed a horn upon the city to keep the residents vigilant against marauding Vikings. It's no wonder that the hornblowing is taken seriously; if it isn't then the ghost of Ripon's first mayor will

The Ripon Hornblower

78

reputedly appear and visit pestilence and tragedy upon the city.

Head along the bottom edge of the market square and down right to the cathedral, where the route bears right. Go straight over a roundabout and then over the river on a latticed metal bridge. Cycle down Bondgate; at a playing field turn right and then immediately left on Knaresborough Road, and then left again on an easy-to-miss turn onto Littlethorpe Road. Use a purpose-built island to cross a busy main road and go straight on to exit Ripon. Do not be disheartened to see a sign telling you the exorbitant distance you have left to travel to York (31 miles/50km). All the big ascents are over and done with and now is the time to get the legs working and power on into Yorkshire's historic county seat.

Continue into the village of **Littlethorpe** and take a right at a small church and then a left at a T-junction sign-posted to Knaresborough. After going under two railway bridges the route leads to **Bishop Monkton**, an attractive village where a stream flows down the roadside and the route turns left towards Boroughbridge. The scenery has now become distinctly arable, with the sheep pastures of the morning having given way to endless fields of crops. Ride straight through the equally attractive **Roecliffe** to cross under the A1 at a roundabout on the outskirts of Boroughbridge. ▶ Go straight across, with the Devil's Arrows standing stones visible immediately on either side of the road. It is worth getting out of the saddle to have a proper look at these.

There is a cycle crossing here but take care.

The Devil's Arrows are a row of three massive monoliths dating from the late Neolithic or early Bronze Age about 4000 years ago. Two stand in a field close to where the Roses route crosses under the A1 near the River Ure at Boroughbridge. The southernmost stone (on the opposite side of the road) is 7m high, making it the second-tallest menhir in Britain and beaten only by the mighty Rudston monolith, which is just over a mile from

Two of the Devil's Arrows at Boroughbridge

the main Roses ride and is passed on Day Ride 5. The stones have weathered to produce peculiar fluting at their tips.

Boroughbridge has the air of a working market town and is pretty but functional. It has far more in the way of amenities than the surrounding villages, and a handful of refreshment and accommodation options. Take a left at a T-junction then go immediately right, followed by another left and immediate right again to pass through St James Square, where the ornate fountain will turn your head. The cobbled Hall Square hosts a war memorial and the open-fronted Butter Market Museum. Head down Aldborough Road, later turning left to **Aldborough** village with its lovely old church of St Andrews, built on the site of a Roman temple. The route goes right past the 3m-high stone battle cross, which commemorates the Battle of Boroughbridge that took place in 1322.

Great Ouseburn takes its name from the source of the River Ouse, which is in the gardens of the old Great Ouseburn workhouse.

The way ahead is straightforward and eventually the route merges onto a larger road at **Great Ouseburn** (shop selling basic provisions). ◄

ALDBOROUGH

Roman mosaic in Aldborough

The Battle Cross at Aldborough stood in the market square at Boroughbridge for over 500 years before it was moved to its current location. This is as close as the Way of the Roses gets to inter-county warfare, being a Yorkshire battle involving a Lancastrian. It commemorates the 14th-century battle of Boroughbridge in which royal pretender Thomas Earl of Lancaster was defeated by his cousin King Edward II's men. Though neither died at the battle, the two men met predictably bloody ends a few years later. Lancaster was drawn, hung and beheaded on his cousin's orders and Edward, who was widely thought a fool by his subjects, was murdered after being imprisoned by his wife and son.

Aldborough is now thought to have been an important Roman town. It was called Isurium Brigantium and was home to the Ninth Legion, as well as being the capital of the Brigantes tribe, who were the largest tribe in Britain and eventually became Romanised. Although only a few small parts of the Roman walls and defences are visible, the village's museum has two lovely intact Roman mosaics which are preserved in their original locations and a collection of artefacts including coins, jewellery and pottery from the site.

Passing the fountain in the centre of Boroughbridge

After the village turn left to Beningborough Hall. A diversion shortly comes in the form of an old wooden toll bridge. There is a very small toll on **Aldwark Bridge** for cars but the good news is that cyclists can cross free of charge (though you may incur the wrath of the bridge-master if you do not come to a complete halt and ask politely to go across).

Aldwark Bridge is one of only eight privately owned toll bridges in the UK. The current relatively sturdy iron and wood bridge replaced one that collapsed and was the scene of a tragedy in 1810, when a group of boys were on the bridge watching river ice going downstream. As they ran to watch from the other side a railing collapsed and 12 boys were drowned, with only one body ever being found.

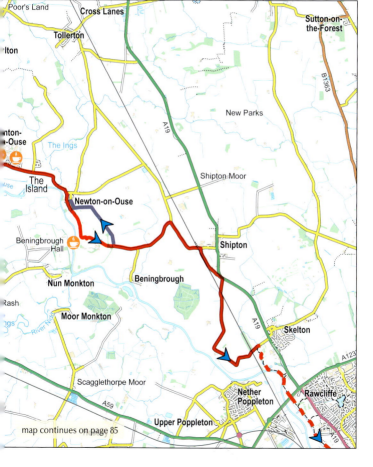

map continues on page 85

Crossing the River Ouse on the rattly wooden slats of Aldwark Bridge

Shortly after the bridge, turn right and continue straight through **Linton-on-Ouse**, watching the skies for planes from the nearby RAF base, and taking a pavement cycle lane for a short section.

> **RAF Linton-on-Ouse** is one of the busiest airfields in the country and – if its website is to be believed – is England's answer to the 'Top Gun' academy, training tomorrow's fast jet pilots for military action.

Beningborough Hall is an Italian-inspired Georgian stately home which houses a collection of paintings from the National Portrait Gallery.

Continue straight on to **Newton-on-Ouse**. Here look out for a right turn which takes you up to the stately home of **Beningborough Hall** (fee if you want to go in the building). ◀ Go in through the grand entrance to the grounds of the hall. There is a good view of the 300-year-old building from the route as it passes the top of the drive, but the house and gardens make a pleasant stop and there is a café at the far side of the hall.

Cycle past the entrance to the tearooms and on out of the grounds to a T-junction. Go right and here and take heart to find that it is now only 6 miles (9.75km) to York. The route next crosses above the East Coast Mainline then turns immediately right (take care). Follow the railway line down the side of a small industrial estate (café). Rather than joining the A19, turn right just before it. Continue across the railway line again at Overton Bridge, where a sign tells passengers it is merely 200 miles to Edinburgh. Go through Overton and under the railway line again to gain the 4-mile (6.5km) cycle path into York, which is signposted right.

> Parts of the route in this vicinity have flooded in the past. If this proves problematic, head through Skelton, crossing the A19 and taking a minor road to Haxby. From here NCN route 23 goes south into York, or you could **bypass the whole flood risk area** by carrying on to Towthorpe then south through Warhill and Holtby. Here the A166 can be crossed and the main Roses route re-joined in Dunnington (see map).

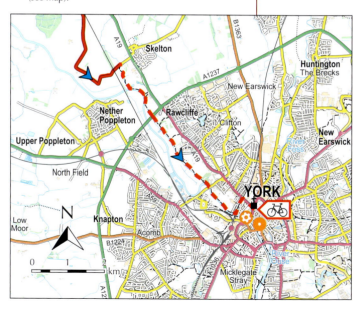

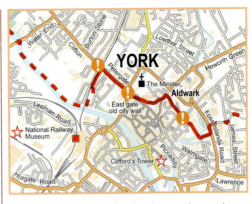

The path is well surfaced and is a welcome change of cycling territory. The route winds down the purpose-built path beside a brook, through meadows and across a metal bridge into woodland, and eventually by the River Ouse. Join a dead-end road for a few hundred metres and then regain the path on the right. There are a few irritating mini cattle grids that shake your weary bones a little at the end of a long day. Go under a main road and eventually emerge near the city centre at a delightful section of riverside walkway with a little marina.

Pay attention to signage for the route where it leaves the embankment after a tunnel under a road bridge and goes up a ramp and a step (dismount necessary), doubling

The riverside path near York city centre

Passing the spectacular York Minster

back on itself for a few metres. Take a cycle path leading up the side of a car-park and under Skelwith rail bridge, then turn immediately right to meet a main road after 200 metres. Take care turning right and use the cycle lane to reach some traffic lights at the **York** city walls. Go straight under the medieval arch of East Gate and suddenly the remarkable York Minster looms right in front of you. Go right up to the Minster to end the day's stage in impressive surroundings.

YORK MINSTER

York Minster is one of the awe-inspiring sites on the Way of the Roses, and to ride up close to its Gothic splendour seems a fitting climax to the day's cycling. The Minster is huge – apparently the whole of Italy's Leaning Tower of Pisa would fit inside its central tower. It hosts a large museum in its Undercroft, and is renowned for its glorious stained glass windows.

A window well befitting the Roses ride

The Minster's Rose Window is particularly symbolic for the Way of the Roses. The outer wheel is made up of a combination of Lancastrian roses and red and white Tudor ones. It is thought to have been designed to commemorate and legitimise the union of the houses of Lancaster and York by the marriage of Henry VII to Elizabeth of York in 1486. A catastrophic fire at the Minster in 1984 led to the ancient glass in the Rose Window being cracked in 40,000 places after being subjected to temperatures of around 450°C. Painstaking renovations were finished three years later, and new bosses around the window were designed by children as young as six who won a *Blue Peter* competition.

EAST TO WEST

The second day is the crux of the route from east to west. Ease yourself out of York on the traffic-free path into a fast flat section to Boroughbridge and Ripon. Most of the really interesting terrain comes in the second half of the day's riding as the route climbs steadily from Fountains Abbey up to Brimham Rocks, followed by an enjoyable section of mainly descent into Pateley Bridge. It is here that the day really has a sting in its tail and a pause to recharge the batteries here is a good idea as going this way means tackling the classic steep climb of Greenhow Hill.

Cyclists must gain nearly 300m of vertical height with sections as steep as an 18% gradient. The initial section is a shock, but there are respites between all the really tough sections and the angle eases towards the top. This is one of the UK's 100 classic climbs; successfully tackling it is a real

Warning sign at the top of Greenhow Hill

incentive to stay in the saddle. It is also safer to stay on the bike as this is a fast and busy road. For those who do get off and push, take heart from the knowledge that even Sir Bradley Wiggins quit the 2016 Tour de Yorkshire shortly after having undertaken the Côte de Greenhow! If this all sounds a bit worrying, take the minor road left just after the start of the hill, passing through Bewerley then turning right up an equally steep minor road that emerges onto the main route by Coldstones Cut. Travelling west, the route does not go through the grounds of Beningbrough Hall. It rather skirts the property on its eastern side.

At Great Ouseburn, it is easy to miss the right-hand fork to Upper Dunsforth, which had no signage in 2017.

A one-way system in Ripon takes westbound cyclists on a needlessly circuitous route from the cathedral to the nearby market place. If you are having a break here, it is far easier to dismount and follow the walking signs left at the cathedral up a short road where the main traffic is pedestrian to reach the market place. The route west is signposted from here, but if in doubt follow road signs for the B6265 towards Pateley Bridge.

DAY 3
York to Bridlington

Start	York city centre SE 603 523
Finish	Bridlington, Headland View, North Marine Drive TA 191 675
Distance	62 miles (100km)
Total ascent	450m
Steepest climb	Millington Dale climb 14%
Terrain	Predominantly minor roads. Cycle path out of York and dirt track for a mile near Stamford Bridge. Two roadside cycle paths.
OS maps	Explorers 294 Market Weighton & Yorkshire Wolds Central, 295 Bridlington, Driffield & Hornsea
Refreshments	Murton, Dunnington, Stamford Bridge, Pocklington, Kilnwick Percy, Millington, Huggate, Kirkburn, Hutton Cranswick, Driffield, Nafferton, Harpham, Burton Agnes, Bridlington
Intermediate distances	Stamford Bridge 10 miles (16km), Pocklington 18 miles (29km), Huggate 26 miles (42km), Kirkburn 32 miles (51km), Driffield 42 miles (68km), Burton Agnes 52 miles (84km)

The miles fly by on this last day of the ride. It seems like a long way to Bridlington, but the gentle terrain of the eastern Vale of York and the Yorkshire Wolds make Day 3 top gear territory most of the way. It is easy cycling unless you are unfortunate enough to encounter the easterly winds that often whip across this flatter land. Whether you have a headwind or a tailwind, however, there is very little freewheeling on today's ride and those hungry for the hills will have to make do with the modest but enchanting climb out of Millington Dale.

A few off-road sections at the start of the day keep the riding interesting as the route heads away from York and into the Yorkshire Wolds at the welcoming village of Pocklington. The Wolds will gain many fans as the Way winds up a superb valley to Huggate and serenely descends through Yorkshire's 'bread basket' to Hutton Cranswick and Driffield. Here the route crosses the Yorkshire Coast railway line seven times as it winds its way up to the Woldgate Roman Road. Cyclists will have the sea in their sights as the route finally makes its way through Bridlington to the more peaceful North Beach promenade with its views of the Flamborough Head Cliffs.

Cycle down the traffic-free area at the right-hand side of York Minster and pass between this and St Michael le Belfry Church, the only challenge being to avoid the numerous inattentive tourists gazing up at the Minster. Pass the Minster School on Godrumgate and – dodging pedestrians – turn right on Aldwark before reaching another breach in the city walls.

This is a peaceful route which leads you out to cross straight over a bigger road and continue traffic free down the left side of a curved glass building and over Hungate Bridge. Turn left after the bridge and then dog-leg left to cross over the A1036 Foss Islands Road and join a traffic-free path signed towards Osbaldwick by a supermarket. ▶ The purpose-built path runs beside a brook and is remarkably pleasant given its urban environment. Where the path T-junctions, turn right towards Murton and Osbaldwick on a slightly rougher surfaced path. Merge left onto a minor road into **Osbaldwick**, where the brook runs on the right hand side of the road. Where the road bends right, keep straight ahead to **Murton**. At Murton go right towards Stamford Bridge, passing the easily missed Yorkshire Museum of Farming with a train carriage visible in its grounds.

Looking back into York city centre, the Minster looms large.

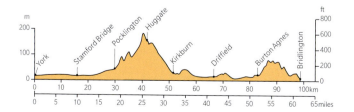

91

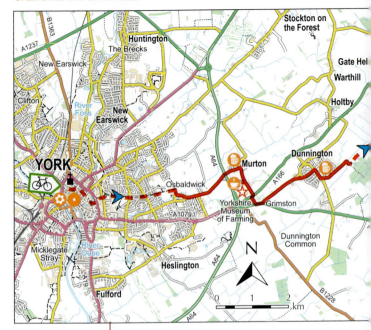

The **Yorkshire Museum of Farming** is a fairly low-key and friendly attraction at Murton Park. Roses cyclists are most likely to stop to make use of its café (Thursday to Sunday), but it does make a good meeting place if you want to check in with a support vehicle after crossing York. The museum hosts livestock and machinery along with an interesting permanent exhibition about the Women's Land Army and an extremely short working railway line manned by enthusiasts.

After 200 metres the road meets the A166. Take care negotiating this at a cycle crossing and continue on in the same direction. After a very brief respite, the route arrives at another busy road – the A1079. Take the pavement cycle path left for less than 200 metres until

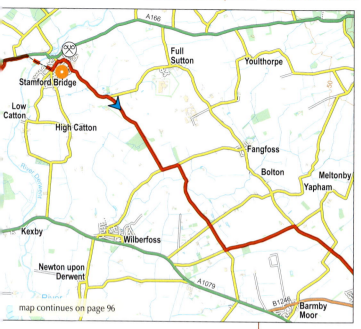

map continues on page 96

veering off left on a quiet lane through **Dunnington** (pub and shop).

At a T-junction turn right, then follow signs doglegging left then immediately right by a small park. The lane is a dead end for cars – it becomes narrower and rough and eventually turns into a dirt track cutting through expansive wheat fields. The track is earthy but does not pose a problem to cyclists on road bikes in all but the very muddiest conditions. Eventually it becomes surfaced once again after Hagg Wood. Before harvest time this is a great part of the route, as wild poppies mingle with the golden crops. The peaceful arable land is interrupted by the A166 again. Here the route cleverly takes a cycle path rightwards through a wooded area to the right of the main road and then rises slightly to cross the River Derwent on a former viaduct.

Cyclists enjoying the off-road section near Stamford Bridge

The Derwent viaduct and Stamford Bridge old station were part of the **North Eastern Railway** between York and Beverley from 1847. The line was another casualty of the widespread Beeching closures of the 1960s.

The railway path takes the Way into **Stamford Bridge**, at the site of the old station. Turn left through the village (all amenities).

A monument close to the route in the village centre commemorates the 1066 **Battle of Stamford Bridge** in which King Harold of England's men defeated and killed his brother Tostig, who was in league with the Vikings. The last great Viking King, Harald Hadrada, also met his death during the proceedings. The most probable site of the actual battle is worth a look. It is 30 metres off route, reached by turning left on White Rose Drive as you leave the village. At the end of the cul-de-sac is a field with a large stone and plaque bearing the graphic details of the battle.

Turn right after St John the Baptist Church on a lovely quiet lane for 2 miles. Dogleg left then right after 500 metres on similarly tranquil roads signposted to Barmby Moor. Look out for a left turn after 2 miles on Toffee Lane, just past a farm on the right (water for thirsty cyclists, with an honesty box). It is here that the higher rolling scenery of the Yorkshire Wolds starts to entice riders onwards. Turn right where you meet a busier road leading into the small market town of **Pocklington**.

Burnby Hall and Gardens are close to the town centre. As well as a small museum, there are two pretty lakes, home to a famous collection of different water lilies and a massive stock of huge carp and roach which enjoy being fed from the hands of visitors.

Head up leftwards into the town centre and into its market place – a good place to rest and refuel with a great deli, café, ice cream shop and pubs. There is also

Memorial commemorating the 1066 battle of Stamford Bridge

Pocklington market place hosts the 2017 Tour de Yorkshire

a small cycle shop here. The route goes left across the bottom of the market place then left on New Street to get out of town. Here Roses riders get their first signage for Bridlington, although it is still an alarmingly long way off. The route soon begins to climb, following signs turning left to the intriguing Kilnwick Percy Buddhist Centre.

Kilnwick Percy is home to the **Buddhist Madhyamaka Kadampa Meditation Centre**. It boasts accommodation and the World Peace café – a stop for cyclists who wish to be enlightened or perhaps practise some positive thinking about the remaining 41 miles (66km) to Bridlington!

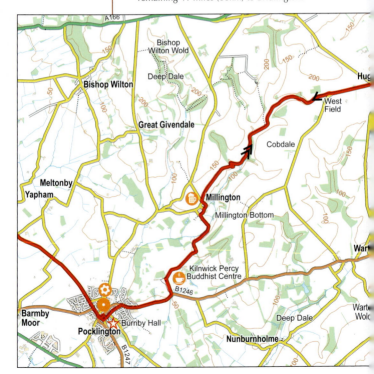

The climb becomes more gradual and heads into immense shimmering hay and wheat fields leading into the pristine village of **Millington**, where the two pubs may catch the eye of cyclists who did not stop in Pocklington. The area is justifiably popular with walkers as well as cyclists.

The Wolds were formed as a result of the last Ice Age 12,000 years ago. The chalk of the Wolds was frozen when the valleys were carved out by icy rivers. As temperatures rose, the chalk thawed and absorbed most of the remaining surface water, creating the dry valleys that the route passes along.

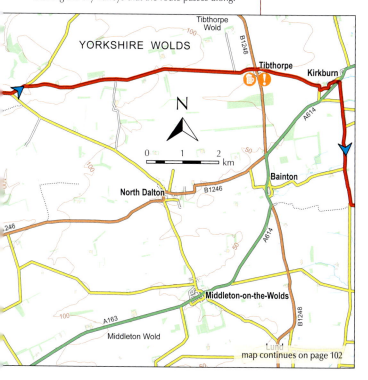

map continues on page 102

The carved wooded posts in Millington Dale

Take care on this gritty and sharply bending descent.

The alluringly named Gypsey Race, which the route crosses on the way into Bridlington, is the only true Wolds stream.

Turn right at the top of the village and, after a gradual climb, descend more steeply into a picturesque valley at Millington Dale. ◄ Riding through the narrow defile of this valley is one of the highlights of the day and will charm cyclists visiting the Yorkshire Wolds for the first time.

The **unusual wooden posts** found in Millington Dale are part of a public art project. The letters on the posts spell out 'Gait in Wolds'. The word 'gait' refers to the historic common grazing land of Millington Pastures. Along with sheep, Highland cattle still graze along the route.

The valley is unusually winding and steep sided and provides superlative cycling. The tiny road eventually climbs steeply out of the dale and the ascent can be surprisingly tiring for weary legs. At the top, merge leftwards onto a wider road and then a fast descent to Huggate (ignore a blue cycling sign pointing left on the 167 here).

Huggate has a pub with rooms and camping (free for those dining at the pub as of 2017 – phone ahead). A mile after Huggate, take the second right forking off to Tibthorpe. At Tibthorpe go straight across a junction onto a fast section of road, where the eagle-eyed might get a morale-boosting first glimpse of the North Sea. After 1½ miles turn left into **Kirkburn** (pub) where there is a war memorial.

Take a road heading right just outside the village and carefully cross the A614. Rise steadily to a junction where a signpost points left (a somewhat demoralising 25 miles/40km to Bridlington). This road climbs gently for 500 metres through the beautiful rape fields of Burn Butts farm. At the top turn left to Hutton Cranswick. Cycling signs at this junction show the distance to Bridlington has now even more disappointingly increased to 26 miles! Continue into **Hutton Cranswick** (passing TJ's coffee shop– which has a large map of the Roses route on its wall – at the garden centre on the way into town). At the

Vast rape fields near Huggate

The old crane at Driffield River Head

main road junction, turn right on a cycle path beside a larger road for 100 metres.

Cross the main road at an easily missed cycle crossing to enter the village centre (shop and pub). At a junction beside the large village green with its reedy pond turn right. Tackle the first of many level crossings on this part of the route and shortly afterwards turn left along a lovely hedged lane.

This road leads northwards through **Skerne** leading in 3 miles (5km) to the outskirts of **Driffield** (or Great Driffield to give it its full name), where the huge red-brick Bradshaw's flour mill looms beside the road and a long mill pond is passed. ◀ Continue on, over a level crossing to a junction. Turn right here, then right again after 50 metres, crossing back over the railway line at a different level crossing. Follow the road past Driffield River Head (actually a canal at this point) where there is a restored old white crane next to the road and a pub and canal-side café. Turn left at the next T-junction, leading over yet another level crossing. Eventually take a right at the next traffic lights. Continue straight on, using a cycle lane on

The way through Driffield needs a little care.

the road past Driffield leisure centre and a cemetery with Commonwealth war graves.

After crossing over a little roundabout, join a segregated cycle lane running alongside a busy road. Where the cycle path ends at a bend, cross over the road to fork right (easily missed) into **Nafferton**. Turn right at the first T-junction to wind through the village where there are several shops and refreshment options. Take care to spot a signed left turn by a large pond and church and take this, winding through more of the village over another level crossing. Fifty metres beyond this, fork left on a straight road (Carr Lane). Less than a mile later take a left turn to Carr House (a dead end for vehicles). This leads to a level crossing without an automatic barrier. Take care here. ▶

After two rights and a left in quick succession you will reach **Harpham** in less than a mile. Turn right up the main street, which has little to lure in tired cyclists.

The residents of Harpham are clearly big fans of **novelty wells**, as there are two in the small settlement. St John's Well is right on route, just before the track to the gated level crossing on the east side of the village. The well water reputedly boosts fertility; cures headaches and eye ailments; and also calms down wild animals. Surely most Roses riders will want to make use of it... The second of Harpham's wells – Drummer Boy's Well – is slightly off route and best avoided as it appears to be the more morbid of the two. Apparently a drum beat issues from the well's depths whenever a member of the local landowner's family is about to die.

Follow Main Street, which turns into a dead-end road leading past St John's Well through a gate onto a track to a gated level crossing (take care again). This is followed by a left turn to yet another level crossing and finally out onto a junction with the A614 by a duck pond at **Burton Agnes** (pub). Turn left on a pavement cycle path, then right after 100 metres to Burton Agnes Hall.

There is a short section of poor road surface in this area, but nothing to worry road bikes.

The waters in St John's Well at Harpham are said to have healing properties

Burton Agnes Hall is an Elizabethan manor house set in beautiful gardens. Its café is popular with cyclists. The hall itself (fee) has some interesting portraits and is supposedly inhabited by a particularly grisly ghost. An ancestor of the current owners asked that when she died, she should be beheaded and her head preserved in the house. When her relatives ignored this request, the haunting began and eventually, driven to distraction, they dug up her grave and embedded her skull in one of the walls, where it remains to this day. Needless to say, all this does not seem to have stopped the ghostly goings on.

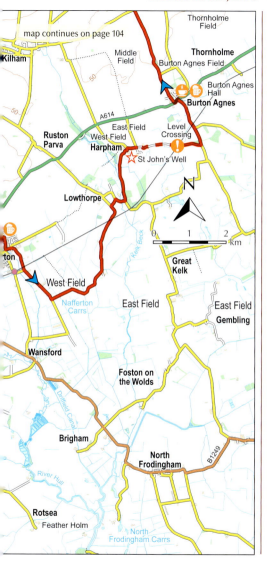

map continues on page 104

Kilham

Thornholme
Field

Middle
Field

Thornholme

Burton Agnes Field

Burton Agnes
Hall

Burton Agnes

A614

Ruston
Parva

East Field
West Field

Harpham

Level
Crossing

St John's Well

Lowthorpe

N

ton

West Field

Nafferton
Carrs

East Field

Kelk Beck

Great
Kelk

0   1   2
km

East Field

Gembling

Wansford

Foston on
the Wolds

Driffield Canal

Brigham

North
Frodingham

B1249

River Hull

Rotsea

Feather Holm

North
Frodingham Carrs

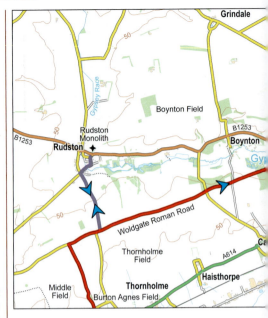

On the last ascent of the ride above Burton Agnes

optional extension map continues on page 110

Here the route is briefly steep up to the hall and then gentler rising through vast wheat and cornfields to the junction with Woldgate Roman road. If energy is running low, console yourself with the fact that this is the last elongated uphill of the route. Turn right and your efforts will be rewarded as the dead straight road gives the first really clear views of the sea.

Detour to the Rudston monolith

A detour of 2 miles there and back can be made to see the Rudston monolith. For further details see Day Ride 6. To get there turn left about 700 metres along the Roman road, from where the village of **Rudston** can be seen in the distance. Descend to a junction near the beginning of the village. Turn right and then immediately right again on Eastgate, over a tiny road bridge with an old water pump. Follow the road leftwards and slightly uphill to

The mighty Rudston monolith

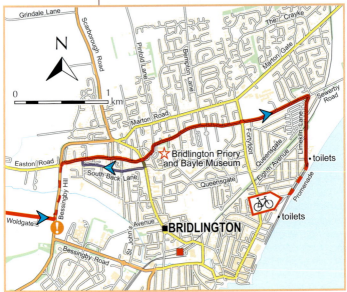

the village churchyard (All Saints' Church) housing the impressive monolith.

> At 8m high, it is the **tallest single standing stone** in Britain and is about 4500 years old. The Neolithic monument is actually a huge piece of moorstone grit – a rock type not found in the near vicinity. One theory is that the monolith was a glacial deposit, but others believe that the massive monolith was transported by ancient humans around 200BC in a mammoth feat of Neolithic engineering. Some researchers also believe that there is an embossed footprint of a dinosaur on the bottom left east-facing side of the stone.

> Retrace your steps to join the main route (do not be tempted to follow the busy B1253 into Bridlington).

The Roman road leads to the outskirts of Bridlington after about 5 miles (8km). As the road descends keep straight ahead, eventually passing through a small wood near the watercourse of Gypsey Race. The town of Bridlington is finally visible ahead. A second descent leads to a further part of the wood which is home to the Woldgate Trekking Centre. ▶ There is one final kick up a micro climb out of a gritty dip.

Look out here for parties of pony trekkers and piles of horse muck on the unevenly surfaced road.

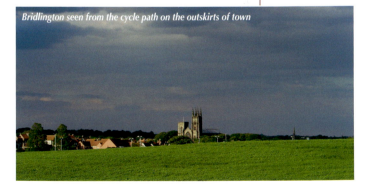
Bridlington seen from the cycle path on the outskirts of town

Where the Roman road emerges onto a main road, turn left on a roadside cycleway that becomes a segregated counterflow cycle lane. Cut right after 300 metres following rose signs through a housing estate to reach **Bridlington**'s Old Town high street. ◄ Go straight across the traffic lights at the junction with St John Street, joining Kirkgate, where the Bayle Museum and the impressive Bridlington Priory can be found.

At this point there is still a fair way to go, but the sound of seagulls crying above you is reassuring.

The arch seen as you enter **Kirkgate** is the Bayle House, originally the 12th-century gatehouse to the priory, formerly used as a prison and possibly once part of a castle. The Bayle House hosts a bargain-priced museum which is surprisingly entertaining, particularly the exhibits chronicling the crimes and misdemeanours of the unsavoury bygone inhabitants of Bridlington, who were imprisoned for anything from throwing dead sheep into the churchyard to letting a woman take unwholesome beef to market.

The imposing Bridlington Priory (free) has beautiful stained glass, a great tapestry showing the history of Bridlington and lots of Robert Thompson's mice carved into the decorative woodwork.

Moody skies above Bridlington Priory

Continue along Sewerby Road, going straight across a small roundabout and then bearing right at the triangular junction after the Headlands School. Here there is a small railway bridge which frames a surprisingly close-up view of the sea. Go under the bridge and head down left off the road onto the beachfront promenade. Go right for 400 metres to find a large sign announcing the end of the route, next to a ramp leading down onto the long and wide North Beach, where the steep white cliffs of Flamborough Head frame the view to the east and the fairground rides of Bridlington's busier South Beach twinkle and swirl further down the coast.

A welcoming sign on Bridlington's North Beach

The beach is usually more sheltered than that of Morecambe and it is an amenable place to finish the ride. The Way of the Roses sign is within striking distance of a café and fish and chip shop, as well as ice cream, souvenirs and public toilets (one set just north of where the Roses route joins the promenade and another set with a drinking water tap 300m south of the finishing sign). There is ample parking along the seafront and nearby streets, and a pedestrian promenade with parks and a crazy golf course. Cycling a mile further south will bring

you to the hustle and bustle of the traditional British seaside resort, complete with all the candyfloss, arcades and waltzers that one could possibly need, if that is the way you choose to celebrate.

Some Roses riders may choose to continue out to finish at the dramatic chalk cliffs of Flamborough Head, 5 miles (8km) further on. To do this, continue along Sewerby Road for another 1½ miles until it meets the B1259. Turn right to the village of Flamborough and continue straight ahead on the same road all the way to Flamborough Head with some sections on roadside cycle path.

FLAMBOROUGH HEAD

The dramatic chalk cliffs at Flamborough Head

There is a café and large parking area here and it's a good spot for gazing wistfully out to sea. There's a fair chance of spotting seals and puffins (in spring and early summer) and a lesser likelihood of catching sight of a Minke whale or porpoise. The headlands have great walking. For those who know their gulls from their gannets there are important seabird colonies here. The site is also of historical interest – Flamborough was the scene of a bizarre sea battle against an American ship in 1779. There are also a few World War II pillboxes in situ along the clifftops.

Flamborough lighthouse itself is functional but also attracts plenty of visitors who climb its 119 steps. The original 17th-century chalk lighthouse is the obvious tower about 200m west of its bigger modern neighbour.

There is plenty to entertain non-cyclists here who may be picking up triumphant Roses riders, along with ample parking, public toilets and a café.

EAST TO WEST

The main ascent of this section is the one to Huggate and it is much more gradual in this direction. There is also a tough little climb out of Millington Dale.

In Bridlington the route is different heading west. It goes from the priory along Kirkgate to turn left on St John's Street for less than 50 metres before turning right on South Back Lane to head out of town.

Take care with route-finding on the section after Burton Agnes through Harpham and Lowthorpe, where the route takes a few twists and turns and signage can be difficult to spot. Driffield also demands concentration as the route takes a very slightly different route in this direction.

There is a one-way system in place around Pocklington market place, but signage is good here and it should not cause any problems.

The Way of the Roses is on route 658 into York centre. Follow signs for the Minster if in any doubt and pick up the rose signs from the front entrance.

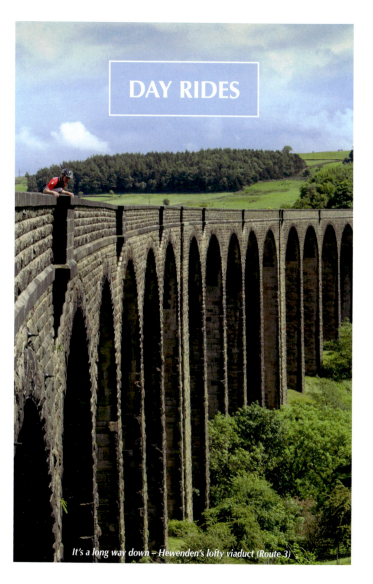

DAY RIDES

It's a long way down – Hewenden's lofty viaduct (Route 3)

ROUTE 1
Arnside and Silverdale tour

Start/finish	Lancaster Castle SD473 620
Distance	40 miles (64km)
Total ascent	600m
Steepest climb	Footeran Lane, Yealand Redmayne 13%
Terrain	Surfaced and gravel canal towpaths, minor roads
OS maps	OL41 Forest of Bowland & Ribblesdale, OL7 The English Lakes – South-eastern Area
Refreshments	Hest Bank, Carnforth, Silverdale, Arnside, Beetham, Yealand, Nether Kellet
Rail	Lancaster, Arnside, Carnforth
Intermediate distances	Warton 9 miles (14km), Arnside 18 miles (29km), Yealand Conyers 27 miles (43km), Carnforth 30 miles (48km)

This is a ride that will bring a smile to any cyclist's face. Heading northwards up the coast from Lancaster through what is justifiably designated an Area of Outstanding Natural Beauty, the ride provides the opportunity to get plenty of fresh sea air into your lungs and enjoy expansive views across Morecambe Bay. The route takes cyclists up and out of the Red Rose county for a brief foray into southern Cumbria with its low-lying fells before heading back into Lancashire through historic villages and superb woodlands.

The route is relatively easy to follow, being entirely on parts of three different National Cycle Network (NCN) waymarked rides. It has a lot of traffic-free sections, all of which are suitable for road bikes.

The route is described as a circuit starting from Lancaster castle, right by the city's train station. Although on-street parking can be found near the castle, motorists can alternatively start from the outskirts of town at the Lune Aqueduct (park on Halton Road at SD 483 640).

From the front of **Lancaster**'s castle facing out, ride left down Castle Hill then split off right down the steep cobbles of Church Street. Turn left on the one-way road (Bridge Lane), then take the first left down Darnside Street to reach the Lune suspension bridge and the Way of the Roses riverside cycle path. Turn right and follow the Roses route for over a mile until the Lune Aqueduct ▶ can be seen above you. Alternatively, from the train station, follow cycling signage for the 6 and 69 to reach the Lune.

Whereas the Roses route continues to follow the Lune at this point, this ride travels above it on the towpath of the canal. To access the towpath, take the ramp up onto the aqueduct from the riverside path. Cross the aqueduct and continue along the canal.

The Lune Aqueduct carries the Lancaster Canal over the River Lune.

A canal boat and its canine crew cross the Lune Aqueduct

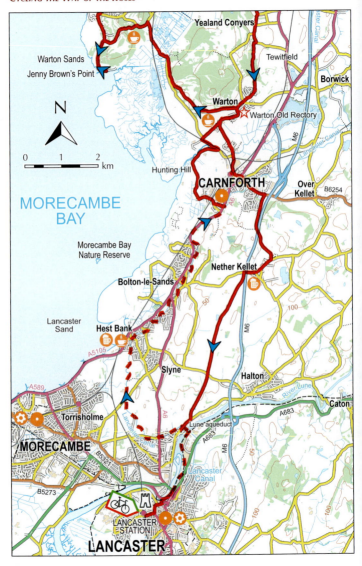

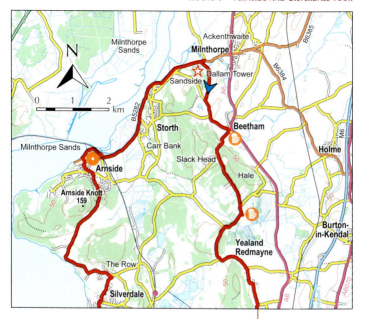

▶ The towpath soon becomes marked as National Cycle Route 6, crossing above the A6 and leaving Lancaster along a lovely stretch of canal, popular with barges and walkers, leading to the pleasant coastal village of **Hest Bank**. Continue on the gently winding towpath past **Bolton-le-Sands**, eventually taking a short section of towpath parallel and close to the A5105 leading into Carnforth. Shortly after a road sign welcoming visitors to Carnforth, look out for easy-to-miss cycling signage for the 700, pointing down a short set of steps to the left. Go down the steps and cross straight over a mini-roundabout following the 700 to Silverdale and skirting **Carnforth** centre on a quiet road.

The 700 is well signed all the way up to Milnthorpe. Continue on the minor road to the village of **Warton** – a great place for a quick stop with cafés, shops and even a microbrewery to its name.

The towpath is tarmacked but by no means smooth and has very short cobbled sections to slow cyclists down as it dips under several low bridges – watch your head.

Warton boasts a 14th-century ruined rectory which is free to look round. The village is famous as the birthplace of the forebears of **George Washington**, America's first president, whose ancestors had a hand in building St Oswald's Church. The Washington coat of arms, which is said to have inspired the design of the USA flag, is on display in St Oswald's and the church still flies the star-spangled banner every year on 4 July.

The 700 turns left in Warton and tackles the first hill of the route, climbing up the wooded flanks of Warton Crag. ◀ Descend across a coastal plain (part of Leighton Moss nature reserve) where the smell of the sea is in the air and the sandy surroundings open up. After a mile turn left towards Silverdale and then 300 metres later left again, overcoming a short rise to reach Gibraltar Farm.

The limestone crag itself can be seen to the right.

Turn left here to get to the lovely picnic spot and coastal lookout of **Jenny Brown's Point**. The short diversion is well worth the effort to gain the rocky seaward edge of the salt marsh. This peaceful spot

At Jenny Brown's Point

is marked by a peculiar tower – probably an 18th-century copper smelter.

From Gibraltar Farm continue onwards for ¾ mile, then taking a right and immediate left into the attractive village of **Silverdale**.

The **Silverdale Hoard**, discovered by a metal detectorist near Silverdale in 2011, is a spectacular collection of Viking coins and jewellery which is on display in Lancaster City Museum.

In Silverdale look out for a sharp left turn towards Arnside on the 700. Enter Cumbria, following a superb stretch of coast and passing right by an enticing beach. The road then bends inland to climb up the lower slopes of Arnside Knott at the treeline. To the right, the medieval ruin of Arnside Tower can be seen. Descend into **Arnside** – another good stopping point with its small port, pier and views north-west to the Lakeland fells. ▶

Keep your eyes peeled for trains crossing the sands on the impressive Kent Viaduct here.

Every month or so, Arnside experiences a mini tidal wave known as the **Arnside Bore**. It is a rare phenomenon where the incoming tide is pushed through a narrow bay causing a wave to travel against the current.

From Arnside seafront carry on up the coast, past the train station, turning left on the 700 towards Milnthorpe.

The route follows the Kent estuary until crossing the River Bela at a bridge just before **Milnthorpe**. ▶ Here this route leaves the 700, taking a tiny private road marked as the 6 through the stone gateposts of a deer park sharply right just before the bridge. The 6 cycle route is followed south to Carnforth. The route goes past **Dallam Tower** country house and its pristine grounds, where fallow deer might be spotted by the eagle-eyed. Exit the park and turn left to reach **Beetham**.

If you reach a sign welcoming careful drivers to Milnthorpe you have gone too far.

At Beetham turn right and ignore an immediate right, instead climbing to Slackhead. Descend through woodland and fork left on the 6. At the next junction ignore signage for the 90 (turning right) and instead go left uphill towards Yealand. At the bottom of the hill go left into Yealand Storrs then continue straight through **Yealand Redmayne** and Yealand Conyers on undulating terrain, eventually dropping through **Warton**, which was visited on the outbound route. Ignore signs for the 6 and 700 and continue straight on through Warton towards **Carnforth**, which is reached shortly thereafter.

On the way into Carnforth, look out for the railway bridge. Ducking right here will take you immediately into the train station with its large clock, instantly recognisable to fans of the classic 1945 film **Brief Encounter**.

Follow Carnforth high street – signposted as the 90 – over a canal bridge. Just before the road reaches the M6 motorway, take a badly signed right to Nether Kellet. This section is rather nondescript but the road is smooth and fast, crossing over the motorway then rising to **Nether Kellet**. Turn right on the 90, then re-cross the M6 and take an immediate left.

More enjoyable riding concludes the ride – staying straight ahead for 5 miles (8km) and eventually dropping onto Halton Road, on the outskirts of Lancaster. Turn right for 200 metres to reach the canal towpath into **Lancaster** at the Lune Aqueduct. Turn right, cross the aqueduct and continue on the Roses route west. At the Lune suspension bridge, look out for cycling signage marking the way back up to the castle and station and the start point.

No time for brief encounters – the famous clock in Carnforth train station

ROUTE 2
The Way of the Dales

Start/finish	Skipton Castle SD 990 520
Distance	49 miles (79km)
Total ascent	1015m
Steepest climb	Brootes Lane, Arncliffe 20%
Terrain	Mainly minor roads, short section of unsurfaced canal towpath (road option available)
OS maps	OL2 Yorkshire Dales – Southern & Western Area
Refreshments	Embsay, Halton East, Bolton Abbey, Appletreewick, Burnsall, Hebden, Grassington, Conistone, Kilnsey, Arncliffe, Malham, Airton, Gargrave
Rail	Skipton, Gargrave
Intermediate distances	Bolton Abbey 6 miles (10km), Kilnsey 19 miles (31km), Arncliffe 24 miles (39km), Malham 33 miles (53km), Gargave 41 miles (66km)

This is a superlative ride with picture-postcard views all the way round. The route showcases some of the gems of the Dales such as Bolton Abbey, Grassington and Malham as well as providing a sense of remoteness in Littondale and on the moors and fellsides near Malham Tarn. A circular trip is made by following the upper reaches of two of Yorkshire's major rivers, up Wharfedale and back via the source of the River Aire into Airedale. The route uses quiet back roads and a short section of canal towpath and starts from the easily accessible market town of Skipton.

From the small roundabout outside the front of the castle, head out of **Skipton** up a road signposted to Embsay. This leads up the side of the castle grounds, past the Bailey car-park. After a few hundred metres turn left on a minor road to Embsay. ▶

Go through the village of **Embsay**, with Embsay Crag visible up left. At the top of the village, turn right towards Halton East. In contrast to the gritstone-topped moors on the left, to your right is the strangely shaped quarried

This is signed with the Swaledale sheep's head denoting the Yorkshire Dales Cycleway.

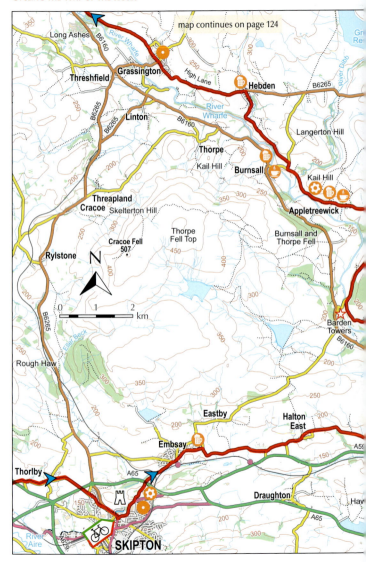

map continues on page 124

Long Ashes

Threshfield

Grassington

High Lane

Hebden

B6265

Linton

River Wharfe

B6160

Langerton Hill

Thorpe

Kail Hill

Burnsall

Kail Hill

Threapland
Cracoe

Skelterton Hill

Appletreewick

Thorpe
Fell Top

Burnsall and
Thorpe Fell

Cracoe Fell
507

Rylstone

N

Barden
Towers

B6160

Rough Haw

Ellen Beck

Eastby

Halton
East

A59

Embsay

Thorlby

A65

Draughton

Hav

SKIPTON

River
Aire

A65

B6265

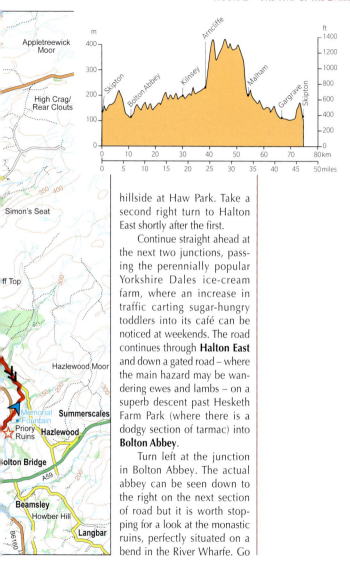

hillside at Haw Park. Take a second right turn to Halton East shortly after the first.

Continue straight ahead at the next two junctions, passing the perennially popular Yorkshire Dales ice-cream farm, where an increase in traffic carting sugar-hungry toddlers into its café can be noticed at weekends. The road continues through **Halton East** and down a gated road – where the main hazard may be wandering ewes and lambs – on a superb descent past Hesketh Farm Park (where there is a dodgy section of tarmac) into **Bolton Abbey**.

Turn left at the junction in Bolton Abbey. The actual abbey can be seen down to the right on the next section of road but it is worth stopping for a look at the monastic ruins, perfectly situated on a bend in the River Wharfe. Go

123

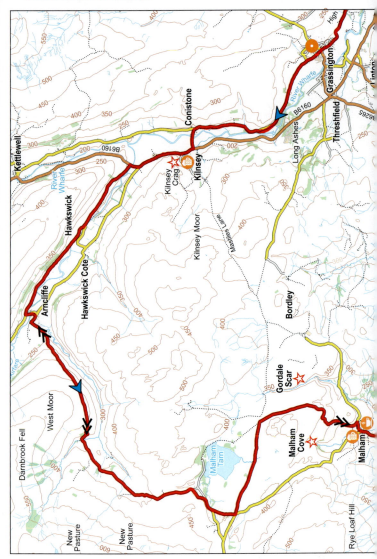

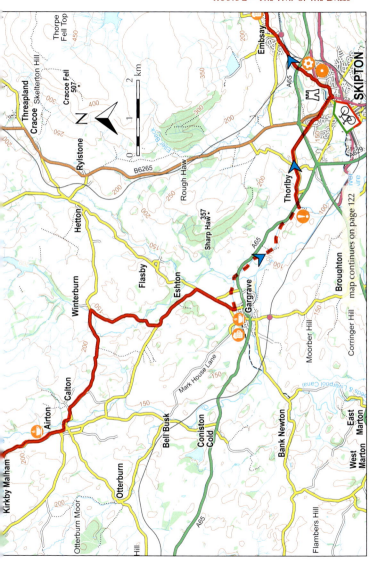

map continues on page 122

Cyclists passing the Cavendish Memorial at Bolton Abbey

There is a booth a short distance away charging car drivers for entry but cyclists can pass freely.

through a narrow stone arch (which has troubled many a 4x4 driver) and continue a few hundred metres to a huge ornate fountain. Here turn right down a private road to Cavendish Pavillion. ◄ At the café by the river, go right over a small bridge and through a gate to access a minor road on the east side of the river.

Turn left and tackle two short but tough rises as the road climbs through woods above the river, and after a couple of miles join the road from Barden Tower. Merge right here towards Appletreewick on another excellent minor road and descend to meet the Way of the Roses route at a T-junction; turn left to go into **Appletreewick** and onwards towards Burnsall. Just before reaching **Burnsall**, look out for a right turn – again marked with the sheep's head cycling sign – towards Hebden. This is followed shortly afterwards by a left turn onto a road which gives the perfect chocolate-box view of the charming Burnsall with its bridge and provides a great section of riding into **Hebden**.

At Hebden take a left towards **Grassington** on a B road.

> **Grassington** is a good place for a stop and has a predictable wealth of cafés and refreshment options on its main street, just up to the right in the centre of the village.

Our route passes the bottom of the main street and after 50 metres turns right at a corner with a large sweet shop, where the main road heads down to cross the river. This is the excellent back road to Conistone, where Wharfedale becomes increasingly craggy and dramatic. **Conistone** is the point at which we re-cross the River Wharfe and begin to head away from it. Follow the main part of the road round left in the village to cross a bridge and briefly turn right on the B6160 at a fairly slow section through the village of **Kilnsey**, passing a trout fishing lake and a pub before heading beneath the impressive overhangs of the **Kilnsey Crag**. The route has now crossed from the gritstone territory of Barden and Embsay Moor into limestone country.

> Kilnsey Crag is a testpiece for **sport climbers**, so expect to spot the odd climber swinging from a rope beneath one of the overhangs on most days.

After Kilnsey, ignore an initial left turn to Arncliffe. Continue on over a bridge and take the second left on a more minor road leading to the same destination. ▶ The scenery is truly spectacular and the route delves into the steeper valley of the River Skirfare. After an initial climb, there is a great stretch by the river with more limestone crags littering the hilltops. Continue through **Hawkswick** to **Arncliffe** (pub). Here go left, dropping over the river. Continue straight ahead on a tiny road, then turn right at the village green.

The road soon bends sharply left beside a small river. The view ahead is of a tremendous climb; it looks daunting but it is exhilarating and truly memorable. The climb

Here the roads are even quieter, as the Dales honeypots of Burnsall and Bolton Abbey are left behind.

The rainbow's end on the Malham Tarn plateau

rises in a couple of steep sections interspersed with more gradual terrain. It is tough but never brutal, and the scenery may make you forget that you're even working hard.

After a level section, there is a briefly exhilarating steep descent down a couple of hairpins bends to a bridge at a farm. Another shorter hill leads up to the plateau of the Malham Tarn area. Watch out for wandering sheep and take in the views of water-worn limestone paving. Eventually the remote tarn itself comes into sight. Look out for a left fork signed to Malham in 3 miles (5km). After 500 metres this leads to a small crossroads. Turn sharp left, as if you are skirting the southern side of **Malham Tarn**, and pass a small chimney on your right. Follow the road, curving right at a wooden signpost and eventually descending into the village of **Malham** (good cafés and pubs, shop). Turn right down into the village. The route heads out left at the T-junction after crossing the river. ◄

The spectacular Malham Cove can be visited on foot by turning right here and following signs for about 20 minutes.

Head out of Malham towards Airton, climbing slightly, with views of the cove behind you. Continue through **Kirby Malham** on to **Airton**. Here the route briefly re-joins the Way of the Roses, turning left following the rose signs in Airton and then right at the top of the rise in **Calton** and continuing on to **Winterburn**. At a humpback stone bridge on a bend (where the Roses route goes left) turn right, heading to **Eshton**. Here join a larger road left to Gargrave. Follow the road into **Gargrave** and look out for a bridge crossing the canal. The route goes left through a gate onto the towpath to avoid the busy and dangerous A65. ▶ The towpath's surface is passable for a road bike but is far from ideal – the majority is grassy with a dirt track. However, it is only necessary to stay on the canal for a short distance and it is by far the preferable route.

A highly inadvisable road option.

It is necessary to dismount where the towpath steeply ducks under the A65, then continue past one farm swing-bridge where there are two gates. Look out for the second bridge – a movable one by a farm – where crossing over left and cycling up a track for 50 metres leads back to the A65.

Dismount and cross straight over onto the road into **Thorlby**. Continue straight on at two junctions in Thorlby and after less than 2 miles reach **Skipton** centre and the castle.

ROUTE 3
Brontë country and the dark satanic hills

Start/Finish	Skipton Castle SD 990 520
Distance	44 miles (71km)
Total ascent	1430m (1600m alt. option)
Steepest climb	Stockshott Lane, Cononley 20%
Terrain	Minor roads, short sections on B roads and cycle path, gravel towpath
OS maps	OL21 South Pennines, small section Explorer 288 Bradford & Huddersfield
Refreshments	Oakworth, Stanbury, Haworth, Oxenhope, Harden, Bingley, on towpath, Silsden, Bradley, Skipton
Rail	Skipton, Bingley
Intermediate distances	Oakworth 12 miles (19km), Haworth 18½ miles (30km), Bingley 31 miles (50km), Silsden 37 miles (60km)

If you don't like it hilly, you would be well advised to avoid this excellent but strenuous ride. However, connoisseurs of Yorkshire's more vertiginous corners (and masochists) will relish this circuit of the Aire Valley. Although it kicks off from Skipton – the 'Gateway to the Yorkshire Dales' – and is only 4 miles (6.5km) from the main Roses route, most of this area has the character of the South Pennines. Expect to find scenery straight out of Emily Brontë's *Wuthering Heights*: brooding moorland, gritstone outcrops (most impressive at Earl Crag) and glimpses of the area's Georgian and Victorian industrial heritage.

The route climbs out of the south side of Airedale, eventually touring the scenic Worth Valley, then descending Haworth's famous steep cobbled high street and climbing over Black Moor to regain the valley floor at Bingley's Five Rise Locks via the spectacular Hewenden Viaduct. The way back follows a canal path to Silsden and undulating minor roads on the moor edges on the northern side of Airedale to Skipton. Alternatively, the majority of the canal section can be avoided by a tough climb. The weather is often wild in this neck of the woods so make sure you check before setting off.

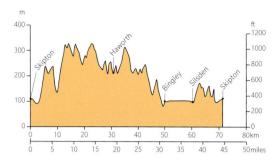

Start from **Skipton Castle** in the centre of town (car-park behind castle on Embsay Road). Go down Skipton's market street, heading straight on at the mini-roundabout at its end. Continue for 600 metres until a traffic light after a petrol station, where you turn right signed to Carleton and Lothersdale. Pass under the railway and after 900 metres look for a left turn after a bridge onto Pale Lane. Continue for 1¼ miles, gaining height and views across Airedale. At the brow of a hill, take the unappealing steep right option towards **Lothersdale** up the unforgiving

Medieval Skipton Castle

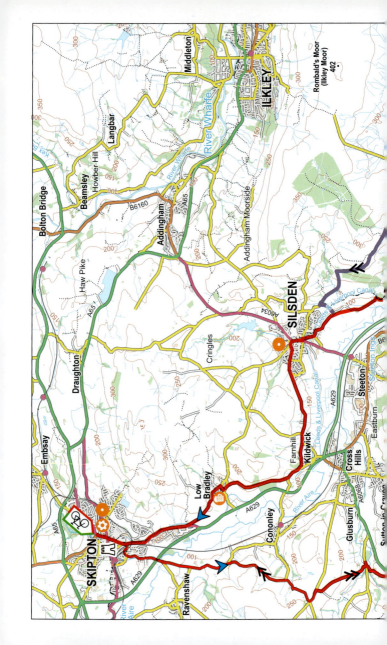

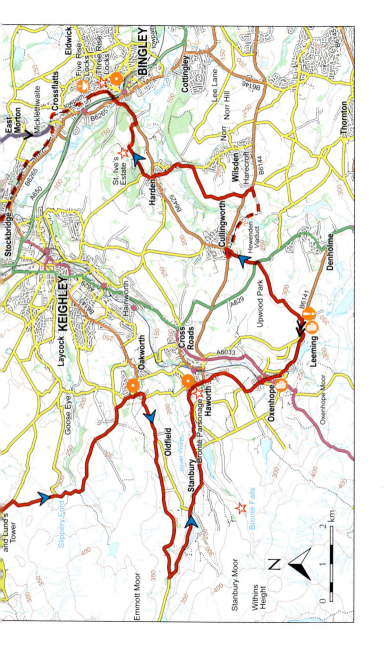

Stockshott Lane. At the top there are views in the distance to the salt- and pepper-pot towers on top of Earl Crag – the next objective.

From here, continue for nearly 1¼ miles, losing some of the gained height (a pattern which will become familiar throughout the day). At a large crossroads, turn left toward Crosshills and Keighley on a wider road, then take the first right after 300 metres (this is not signposted to anywhere). This is a reasonably steep but fast descent, until a bend at its bottom. The next directions to remember are right then immediately left, then right then immediately left again after a brief interlude to cross Holme Beck. It is easier than it sounds, particularly as **Earl Crag** is now looming. The memorable Dick Lane leads up at

On the steep cobbles of Haworth's main street

a relatively amenable and enjoyable gradient across the bracken-scented hillside, passing just beneath the striking **Lund's Tower** at the crag's far end. ▶

From the top of the climb, continue for more almost ¾ mile, ignoring a first crossroads, to take a right turn opposite a farm to the intriguingly named **Slippery Ford**. The route continues on this road for nearly 2½ miles. It trends down to cross Dean Beck (not at a ford thankfully) and climbs over White Hill to eventually reach the outskirts of **Oakworth**. Here take notice of blue cycling signage. Turn right on Wide Lane, immediately past a cemetery, then right at every junction (four) thereafter following blue signs. This eventually leads you out of Oakworth to a climb up Denby Hill Lane. Follow this road for just over 3 miles (5km), gaining height, crossing the Pennine Way and looking across the Worth Valley to Brontë Falls and Ponden Reservoir.

At a junction with a wider road, turn sharply left to Haworth. Continue on undulating territory through Stanbury and into **Haworth**. At the Brontë Parsonage museum (home of the famous literary sisters) fork right, quickly reaching the cobbles of Haworth's uniquely charming main street.

▶ The 2014 Tour de France riders rode up the horrendously steep cobbles (20% maximum) but thankfully we descend, taking a right turn to Oxenhope when the cobbles end. After just over a mile, take a left to Oxenhope down Moor Side Lane and eventually into **Oxenhope**, bearing left onto the main road through the village. Go right at the mini-roundabout towards Denholme. Pass a mill chimney and start a vicious climb up through **Leeming** to the Dog and Gun pub. At the pub, take a left on Trough Lane to Cullingworth via some surprisingly flat ground. This road emerges at the busy A629. Cross leftwards and go down Manywells Brow towards Cullingworth. ▶

Descend Manywells Brow to a mini-roundabout and go straight across. After 50 metres turn left on New School Lane past a primary school onto the traffic-free Great Northern Railway Trail, doubling back to cross

Lund's Tower was built in 1887. It is possible to climb the spiral staircase to the viewing platform of this Victorian folly. There is no entrance charge.

If you're looking to stop and pick up a vegan pasty, a pair of clogs or a herbal remedy, then this is the place for you.

This is the most dangerous junction on the route, so it's best to dismount and use the pedestrian crossing.

The view of Hewenden Viaduct from Bents Lane

Hewenden Viaduct is one of the tallest rail bridges in the country. Some of its 17 stone arches are 37m high.

the railway bridge that the route passed under on the way into the village. The railway path gives views of Hewenden reservoirs and then crosses the immense **Hewenden Viaduct** (take a look by the information sign before you cross). ◄

The path soon ends at a gate where a track leads onto a road and a short climb to **Harecroft**. At a junction turn left on the main road for 200 metres ensuring you don't miss Bents Lane, on which turn right at the brow of a hill. This gives superb views of the viaduct and a narrow, technical descent. Turn left where it emerges on Harden Lane, eventually climbing on a B road to reach a mini-roundabout. Here go left and immediately right. Head uphill steeply for 200 metres to reach the entrance to **St Ive's Estate**, by means of a right turn on a **hazardous corner**. Go through the pleasant estate, blooming with rhododendrons in summer. The main estate road emerges onto a B road, which is followed left on a quick descent to **Bingley**. At the traffic lights in Bingley look almost straight across the main road (turn left then right) to find a ramp up to a narrow footbridge (permissible to cycles) which leads across the A road in the valley floor and leftwards up onto the towpath of the Leeds & Liverpool Canal at **Three Rise Locks**. Go along the towpath and shortly afterwards up a paved steepening beside the colossal **Five Rise Locks**, which was built in 1774. It's a surprisingly spicy little climb, but spare a thought for any beleaguered bargees too. ▶

Here cyclists who have had enough can quit and return to Skipton by train from the nearby Bingley rail station.

Five Rise Locks negotiates the steepest section of canal in the UK. It is a staircase lock allowing a boat to gain over 18m of height in five stages over 98m, making it a 1:5 gradient!

After a patchy start, the towpath surface is very good, fast and wide. Follow it until the second road bridge at **Crossflatts**.

This is **Morton Swing Bridge** with a canal level crossing, a mile marker 'Leeds 17¼ miles, Liverpool 110 miles' and a cycling sign marking 'Riddlesden 10 min'. A sign welcoming drivers to Crossflatts is visible on the road down to the left.

There are now two options:
Option 1 Continue on the canal towpath on a reasonable surface through farmland and woodland for another 4 miles (6.5km). Look out for a black-and-white

The impressive canal engineering at Bingley's Five Rise Locks

stone bridge with a farm track on it at a bend in the canal. Here there is a sign for an angling club and a visible farm to the left. The tarmac surface of the towpath stops under the bridge, so if you find yourself cycling on rutted mud, you have gone too far. The farm is called Lower Holden Farm. Carry your bike down four stone steps onto the farm track (a permissible cycle route) and swing right through the farm onto a concrete track which becomes the tarmacked Low Lane, then Hainsworth Road. Follow this for almost ¾ mile until you are greeted with a cul-de-sac sign. At the sign, fork left (spotting cycling signage on a lamppost) and dip under the canal. Turn left to reach **Silsden** high street.

Option 2 From Morton Swing Bridge, cross the canal and go up the hill into **East Morton**. At the village's mini-roundabout, turn left then immediately right on Street Lane marked Silsden 5 miles (8km). Continue to ascend, then savour the level section where the views across to Earl Crag are good and just about justify the 170m vertical height gain from the canal. Descend steeply and with care towards Silsden. As the road flattens out, look out for an easy-to-miss sharp left turn just before a small electrical substation where there is a small triangle of grass and a sign marked unsuitable for HGVs and showing a canal bridge. This narrow lane leads down to the canal and crosses Brunthwaite Bridge. Turn right shortly afterwards into Silsden on Hainsworth Road and follow the description for Option 1 above into **Silsden**.

In **Silsden**, turn right along the high street for 200 metres and go left immediately after a church, then 50 metres later left again on Skipton Road. It's straight ahead to **Kildwick**, but there's another climb to get there. Pass stately Kildwick Hall and head right to Bradley up yet another hill past a lovely silver birch wood.

At **Low Bradley**, take the first left down Matthew Lane towards the distinctive mill chimney then right to a junction at the village shop. Go left uphill for mercifully the final time. The climb alongside lovely moorland leads down to a roundabout where a right turn eventually gains Skipton town centre and the starting point.

ROUTE 4
Otley and Knaresborough round

Start/finish	Otley market place SE 204 454
Distance	46 miles (74km)
Total ascent	960m
Steepest climb	Moor Lane, Askwith 10%
Terrain	Minor roads and cycle paths, short section on a B road
OS maps	Explorer 298 Nidderdale
Refreshments	Askwith, Birstwith, Ripley, Knaresborough, Spofforth
Rail	Knaresborough, Pannal
Intermediate distances	Askwith 3½ miles (6km), Birstwith 17 miles (28km), Ripley 21 miles (33km), Knaresborough 25 miles (41km), Spofforth 32 miles (52km)

This is an extremely gratifying circular ride linking two of Yorkshire's historic market towns which were both key staging points on the 2014 Tour de France and have links to world champion women cyclists. Lizzie Deignan (Armistead) grew up in Otley, whereas the formidable Beryl Burton (who rode for Knaresborough Cycle Club late in her career) gave her name to the excellent cycleway used on this ride. The route takes high moorland over to twin reservoirs, then goes on superb cycle paths via three castles and returns past another Yorkshire landmark, Almscliff Crag. You will see plenty of bikes per mile as the area is hugely serious about its cycling and Otley has hosted its own prestigious road race for more than 30 years.

The route is located a few miles south of the main Roses route; it is easy to connect to the parent route by going north on minor roads from Birstwith. The terrain is mainly minor roads with a long section of multi-use surfaced path between Birstwith and Knaresborough. The more populated zone around Harrogate means necessity dictates that a few stretches on slightly faster roads and the crossing of three A roads are necessary. It's a fairly taxing undertaking, with the toughest climb at the start of the day.

From the top of **Otley** market place (where there is a stone clock) follow the road sign for Pateley Bridge and

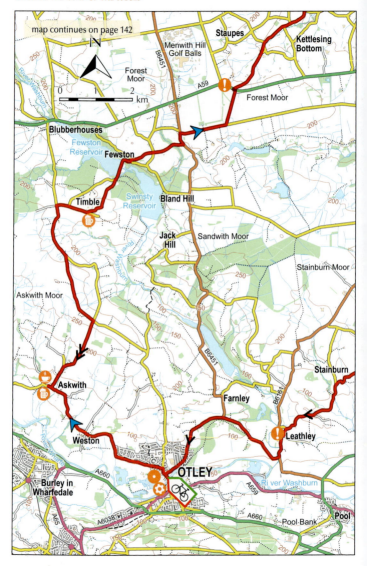

map continues on page 142

N

Staupes

Kettlesing Bottom

Menwith Hill Golf Balls

B6451

Forest Moor

A59

Forest Moor

0   1   2
km

Blubberhouses

Fewston Reservoir

Fewston

Swinsty Reservoir

Bland Hill

Timble

Jack Hill

Sandwith Moor

Stainburn Moor

Askwith Moor

River Washburn

150

100

50

150

B6451

250

Stainburn

100

Askwith

Farnley

B6161

Leathley

Weston

100

100

OTLEY

Burley in Wharfedale

A660

A65

A6038

Pool Bank

Pool

River Washburn

A659

A660

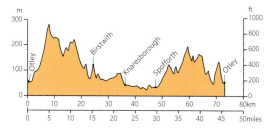

Farnley. The road winds down across a bridge over the River Wharfe, where there is a park and a weir. After the bridge take the first major left turn onto Weston Lane. This is a popular stretch for cyclists and soon begins to climb to the hamlet of **Weston** (café) and on to **Askwith** (pub). Go through most of Askwith then take the road right signed to Blubberhouses and Pateley Bridge – this is a steep but gratifying pull up to Denton Moor and into the Nidderdale AONB.

Turn left where the road meets a wider one, giving views rightwards to the surreal looming golf balls of Menwith Hill. After 2 miles turn right to Timble. Stay right on a lane at a fork 300 metres later to take a gravelly descent into the hidden village of **Timble**. This leads down to cross the dam between the pretty twin reservoirs of Fewston and Swinsty. ▶

About 200 metres after the dam turn left uphill towards Pateley Bridge. Continue straight across the first crossroads then, after another 800 metres, turn left at a T-junction on a B road towards Pateley Bridge. At the first opportunity, turn right signed to Harrogate. It is fast cycling territory here, so don't miss taking the first unsigned left turn after a mile which leads up to the A59. Carefully cross this and continue in the same direction (actually left then immediately right) into the curiously named **Kettlesing Bottom**. Here follow signs rightwards to the lovely village of **Birstwith** (church, shop and pub).

At Birstwith take the road right downhill by the post office to meet a section of signed cycleway into **Ripley**. This is well surfaced and exceptionally pleasant.

There are public toilets at the car-park here.

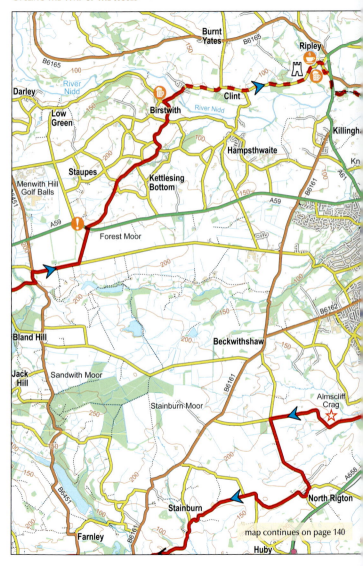

Burnt Yates

B6165

Ripley

Darley

River Nidd

B6165

100

Clint

Birstwith

River Nidd

Low Green

150

Killingh

Staupes

Hampsthwaite

150

Kn

A61

Menwith Hill Golf Balls

Kettlesing Bottom

100

A59

B6161

6451

A59

Forest Moor

200

B6162

Bland Hill

200

Beckwithshaw

150

Jack Hill

Sandwith Moor

B6161

Almscliff Crag

Stainburn Moor

250

North Rigton

A658

B6451

Stainburn

150

map continues on page 140

Farnley

100

B6161

Huby

map continues on page 140

142

On the path leading past Ripley Castle

It eventually brings you to Ripley's 14th-century castle (fee to visit). The bridleway and the following Nidderdale Greenway are justifiably popular with families at the weekends and due care should be taken when passing slower parties. This is a good place to take it easy. The pristine village of Ripley has all amenities and public toilets on route.

Bear right for 50 metres on the road at Ripley to then follow the signed Nidderdale Greenway (NCN 67) through undulating woodland as far as a minor road crossing at **Old Bilton** where a left turn must be taken. This leads onto the Beryl Burton Cycleway after 500 metres.

Beryl Burton overcame chronic childhood illness to win seven world cycling titles in the 1960s. In 1967 she set a 12-hour time trial record of 277¼ miles (446km), beating the men's record in the process. No man could beat her distance for more than two years and no woman has done so yet.

The surfaced path provides pleasant leisurely cycling into the impressive Nidd gorge at Knaresborough and brings cyclists out directly opposite the entrance to the eccentric Mother Shipton's Cave. ▶

Mother Shipton's Cave is worth a short visit to see the junk which has been suspended in the dripping water to calcify – this even includes a bike! This is supposedly England's oldest tourist attraction, the birthplace of an ancient soothsayer who foretold the Great Fire of London and the defeat of the Spanish Armada. Turn left for 100 metres on the main road at **Knaresborough** and then turn right down Waterside along the riverbank, where good cafés abound and numerous tourists gather for boating and strolling. Follow the riverside gorge route under the impressive cliffs housing the castle, crossing the B6163 and after another mile turning right on the B6164 (roadside cycle lane). This leads in 300 metres to two unappealing busy roundabouts – go straight across both to Little Ribston. The road improves and leads to **Little Ribston** in 3 miles (5km). Here turn right to **Spofforth**.

> **Spofforth Castle** is free to enter. The present ruins are from the 14th century, but a manor house existed on the site long before that – reputedly the place where the Magna Carta was drawn up.

Turn right in the village centre (NCN route 67) past the castle to Follifoot. Go left in **Follifoot** and look out for cycling signage leading you onto a short and often muddy underpass of the A658. When this emerges head left to **Pannal**. Here another A road is crossed with care. Go straight ahead down through the village past the railway station.

It can be confusing getting on the right road from Pannal. The simplest way is by circumnavigating the village. About 400 metres after crossing the river go left uphill on Spring Lane. After 900 metres turn left again at a mini-roundabout on Burn Bridge Road, then at a second little roundabout keep left on the same road. After

Knaresborough and its ruined medieval castle seem to cling to the side of the Nidd gorge. The route passes under an impressive towering viaduct on its way through the town.

On the road past Almscliff Crag

It would be unusual not to see some climbers testing their mettle on this popular and famously harsh gritstone outcrop.

descending back over the river finally turn right up Hill Foot Lane and eventually onto moorland again.

At the first major crossroads bear left to **North Rigton**. In North Rigton go right and right again on Crag Road leading up to skirt the foot of **Almscliff Crag**. ◄ Fork right just before the car parking for the crags.

Follow this road all the way through the villages of **Stainburn** and **Leathley**. In Leathley turn left downhill, then after 600 metres right uphill again towards **Farnley**. Continue for about 5 miles (8km) to reach the bridge over the River Wharfe at **Otley**. Turn left to reach the starting point.

ROUTE 5
Around the Wolds in a day

Start/finish	Huggate SE 882 550
Distance	47 miles (76km)
Total ascent	871m
Steepest climb	Horse Course Lane, Settrington 12%
Terrain	All on minor roads
OS maps	Explorers 300 Howardian Hills & Malton, 294 Market Weighton & Yorkshire Wolds Central
Refreshments	Huggate, Thixendale, Leavening, Malton/Norton, North Grimston
Rail	Malton
Intermediate distances	Thixendale 10 miles (16km), Malton 30 miles (48km), Duggleby 42 miles (68km)

This challenging loop takes you through the heart of the High Wolds. The chalk escarpments, dry valleys and pretty villages which characterise the area abound, and the cycling is mainly on very quiet single-track lanes through an area steeped in history where the traces of Neolithic farmers, medieval settlers and monks can be uncovered. The route includes Malton (though an optional bypass of the busy market town is also described) allowing access to the loop by train.

For those accessing the start by car, park at Huggate on the road. Be warned, this area can be very windy. On breezy days, the crosswinds on the High Wolds can make this ride feel much harder than it appears on paper.

Follow the Way of the Roses out of **Huggate** in the direction of Millington for roughly 200 metres until there is a signpost right for NCN route 167 to Malton. After roughly 3 miles (5km) take the first left towards Millington on a wider road, and continue for a mile until a long bend where the 167 to Malton is marked sharply right. Take this, almost doubling back on yourself at first.

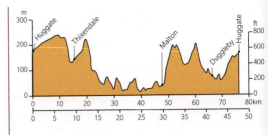

On reaching the main road, go left on the cycle path for 300 metres then cross over carefully and head up a minor road to Thixendale (marked 167). Look out for the easily missed second right turn. Take this on a gentle downhill stretch to Thixendale. The scenery is open and arable with views to the High Wolds and a colourful

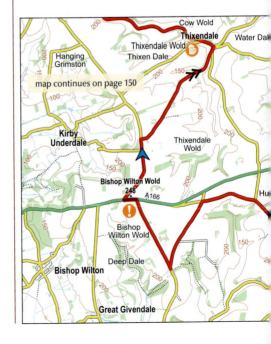

map continues on page 150

patchwork of fields and valleys spreading out before you. Pass the North Yorkshire sign and drop down steeply past the Robert Fuller wildlife art gallery into **Thixendale** via a charming sinuous Wolds valley. At the bottom of the hill turn left into the village (shop, pub).

From Thixendale, wind up through Water Dale with **Cow Wold** on your right. ▶ Climb out of the valley to **Aldro Farm**, keeping straight ahead and going straight across a small crossroads marked to Leavening.

With the gained height come expansive views north across the lower land to Malton. Descend steeply to **Leavening** and turn right out of the village on Malton Road (167, Malton 6 miles/9.5km). At the bottom of a downhill stretch turn left to Westow, still on the 167, and follow a great single-track grassy lane with a slightly dubious road surface, going straight across at the next junction. At

This is aptly named as Highland cattle are farmed on its slopes.

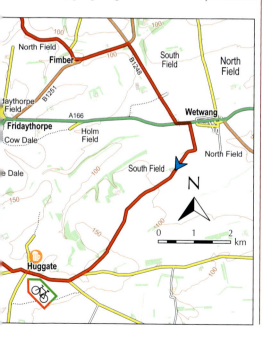

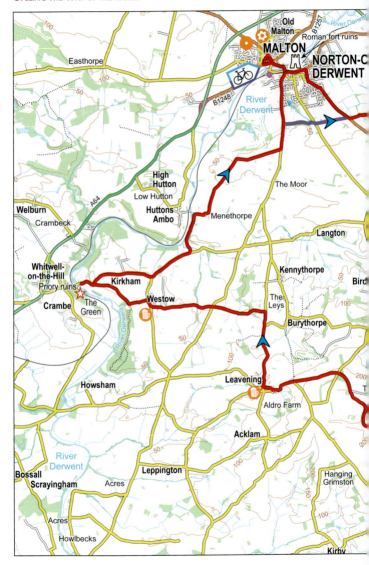

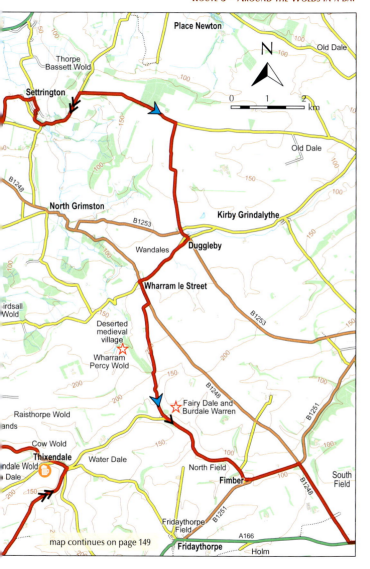

Place Newton

Old Dale

Thorpe
Bassett Wold

Settrington

N

0   1   2
km

Old Dale

B1248

North Grimston

Kirby Grindalythe

B1253

Wandales

Duggleby

Wharram le Street

B1253

irdsall
Wold

Deserted
medieval
village
Wharram
Percy Wold

B1248

Fairy Dale and
Burdale Warren

B1251

Raisthorpe Wold

ands

Cow Wold

Thixendale

ndale Wold

Dale

Water Dale

North Field

Fimber

South
Field

B1248

Fridaythorpe
Field

B1251

map continues on page 149

A166

Fridaythorpe

Holm

151

The ruins of Kirkham Priory

a stone cross in **Westow** village go right, then left shortly afterwards, still following the 167 signs to Kirkham.

At the top of the village of **Kirkham** (pub), take note of a sign marking the 166 rightwards. This will be our continuation after a very short but worthwhile detour down into the village to see Kirkham Priory. Stop at the priory and bridge, then turn around to return up the short hill to go left on the 166.

> **Kirkham Priory** was founded in the 12th century on the banks of the River Derwent. Its gatehouse is remarkably intact. The priory was the location for a secret meeting between Winston Churchill and King George VI when troops were training in the village during the run up to D-Day, even using clambering nets to practise scaling the ruined walls.

To avoid Malton turn left at the T-junction, then right on the 166 to Hunmanby. Keep straight on at two junctions to cross the B1248; re-join the main route on the lane to Settrington.

Climb out of Kirkham on the 166 then descend gently and filter left onto a better-surfaced road and wind down, branching left again on the 166 to Menethorpe at a dip, then briefly following the River Derwent. Turn left at a T-junction towards **Malton**. ◀

Cross a railway line and the river, then follow the road for 300 metres. At the first set of traffic lights turn left on Yorkersgate and take the second right into the attractive market square.

> **Malton** is a good choice for a lunch stop as the town prides itself on being the foodie capital of North Yorkshire. The remains of the town's Roman fort – known as Derventio – and the Castle Gardens are also in the heart of the town and well worthy of attention.

Leave Malton market square by its top right corner (looking uphill) and head down Finkle Street. Turn right on Newbiggin, eventually re-crossing the river and railway and following road signs for the B1248 to Beverley heading out of town.

After another 1¼ miles on the B1248, turn left on the 166 to Settrington on quiet lanes once again. ▶ Turn left once again at a dip by Sparrow Hall, then follow the road round right into **Settrington**. Go over a bridge and past the village hall and then take a right turn signed 166, on a dead-end road. Follow the 166, turning right again shortly afterwards down to a ford where there is also a cycle-friendly bridge for those who don't fancy getting splashed. After 100 metres, merge left onto a minor road and then take a left towards Settrington House. There is a surprisingly long steep climb up from the stately home. Turn right on the 166 to Duggleby, climbing more gently with wide-ranging views once again. After 2 miles turn right again before a descent into Duggleby.

The route follows NCN route 166 all the way to Duggleby from here.

In **Duggleby** go straight on at a crossroads. ▶ Turn right after 200 metres to Wharram Percy, filtering left after a further 200 metres. At **Wharram-le-Street** turn left up the B1248 for 600 metres, then right to Wharram Percy. This road takes you past the remains of a medieval village (a 15-minute walk from the road), before descending a steep and spectacular section of narrow tarmac on the Chalkland Way, passing the chalky cliffs of Fairy Dale

Our route leaves the 166 here, but route-finding is still simple.

and Burdale Warren before commencing a gentler stretch into Fimber.

Wharram Percy medieval village was occupied roughly from AD900 to 1500. Forced evictions led to its abandonment but the medieval church is intact, along with the grassy foundations of nearly 50 other buildings. The site is now managed by English Heritage but is free to visit.

After a small climb to **Fimber**, turn left for a mile to meet the B1248 at a roundabout. Go right here towards the amusingly named **Wetwang**. At a T-junction with a main road turn left for 200 metres then right on a minor road, which leads all the way back to the starting point at **Huggate**.

Prehistoric man seems to have favoured the fertile chalky soil and good grazing of the Wolds. Flints and axes from this period have been found in this area. The mound of **Duggleby Howe**, one of the largest round barrows in Britain, is visible from just beyond the turn-off to Wharram in Duggleby. There are also medieval earthworks en route at Settrington.

ROUTE 6
Bridlington to Scarborough extension

Start	Bridlington TA 177 680
Finish	Bridlington Priory, Scarborough North Beach TA 045 884
Distance	26½ miles (43km)
Total ascent	350m
Steepest climb	Danebury Manor climb, Fordon 8%
Terrain	Minor roads, short sections of cycle path
OS maps	Explorer 301 Scarborough, Bridlington & Flamborough Head
Refreshments	Burton Fleming, Flixton, Cayton, Scarborough
Rail	Scarborough
Intermediate distances	Rudston 10 miles (16km), Burton Fleming 14 miles (22.5km), Flixton 20 miles (32km)

This is the only one-way day ride in this guide, the idea being that the return leg is made by the direct train link between the two towns. As well as being a great day ride in its own right, the route also has considerable merit as an extension or even alternative finish to the Way of the Roses. Heading inland brings you into Wolds territory, going north on surprisingly peaceful minor roads towards the historic spa town of Scarborough.

From **Bridlington Priory**, go out of the town following Way of the Roses signs. Confusingly, there is a one-way system in place on the route, meaning that the outbound course turns left on St John's Road and almost immediately right. This leads out of town through a housing estate to an A road. Go left on the cycle path next to the road for a few hundred metres and then carefully cross the road

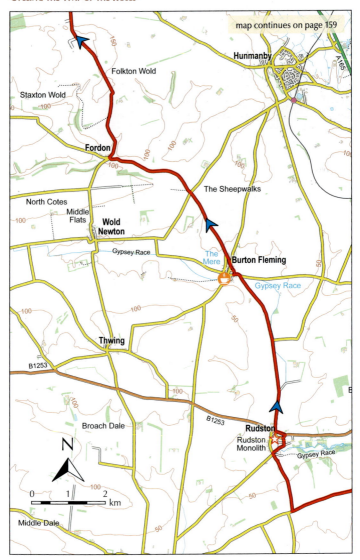

map continues on page 159

Hunmanby

Folkton Wold

Staxton Wold

Fordon

The Sheepwalks

North Cotes

Middle Flats

Wold Newton

Gypsey Race

The Mere

Burton Fleming

Gypsey Race

Thwing

B1253

B1253

Broach Dale

Rudston

Rudston Monolith

Gypsey Race

N

0   1   2 km

Middle Dale

and go right, signposted Way of the Roses and Woldgate Trekking Centre. This lovely wooded lane was formerly a Roman road. It dips down in the vicinity of the trekking centre and cyclists should take care of horses and a sketchy road surface on this stretch.

Continue for more than 4 miles (6.5km), taking the second right turn (at a give way sign on a bend in the road). The Way of the Roses goes straight ahead but our route turns right down into Rudston – the village church can be seen from here. The scenery now becomes arable and it is mainly freewheeling into the village. Look out for a World War II Nissen hut on your right by the welcome sign for **Rudston**. ▶

Rudston claims to be the oldest continuously populated village in Britain.

At a junction near the beginning of the village turn right and then immediately right again on Eastgate, over a tiny road bridge with an old water pump. The road bends left and continues slightly uphill, eventually leading up to the village church. Stop here to see the impressive Rudston monolith (see Day 2 Burnsall to York).

From the church, turn left down the main road for less than 100 metres then take a right signposted to **Burton Fleming**. The road passes through gentle arable land and then forks left at a junction coming into the village, where the Gypsey Race flows alongside the main street (pub and café). Turn right on Back Street past the attractive village duck pond to emerge at St Cuthbert's Church – parts of this building date from Norman times. Take the left-hand fork past the church signed to Fordon. Here the scenery becomes less flat and more Wold-like in character.

At a crossroads after 1½ miles go straight on and enter a steep-sided Wolds valley which winds its way into the tiny hamlet of **Fordon**. Turn right here to Flixton, climbing up on a single-track road through another typical Wolds valley. Continue to climb, gaining extensive views to Scarborough (although not the sea) at the top. The descent from here is **very steep** so take care as there is a tight left-hand bend at the bottom.

In the Wolds between Burton Fleming and Fordon

As you come into **Flixton**, look out for a right turn on Back Lane just before reaching the main road. Take this until it re-joins the main road, then turn right and

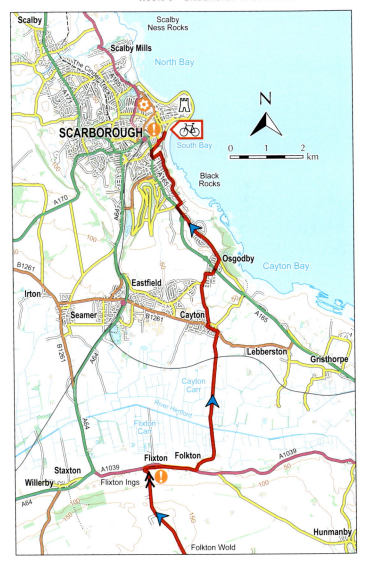

Scarborough's South Bay and the clifftop castle

follow the main road for less than 500 metres through the village. At a sign welcoming you to **Folkton**, turn left on NCN route 1, which is now followed all the way into Scarborough. The road winds down past a church and continues on fast ground towards **Cayton**. At Cayton go over a level crossing and then turn left at a T-junction. Take the third right at the top of a small rise by another pretty church, signed as cycle route 1 to Scarborough. This leads into Osgodby on a minor road.

Go straight on through **Osgodby**, dipping to cross a bridge over an A road, and then turn left at a junction at the top of the village. Scarborough town centre is sign-posted on route 1. From here there are great views of Scarborough's cliffs, grand seafront buildings and sweeping sands.

Just before the road from Osgodby joins a big roundabout head right, following cycling signs, on a short section of traffic-free path that brings you up beside the main road into **Scarborough**. After a short distance, keep your eyes peeled for the blue cycling signs. Turn right on Wheatcroft Avenue, then take a left at the first junction downhill and then right at the bottom of the hill on Esplanade Crescent, staying on the roads nearest the coast. Pass the pristine South Cliff gardens, which are a great place to explore. Route 1 goes left at Albion Gardens through grand terraces and past a church, then turns right. Before the lofty road bridge that crosses the huge gorge of the bay, cut down right onto the seafront proper and the South Beach.

Scarborough straddles two sandy bays, with its 11th-century castle sitting atop the rocky promontory that divides them. The South Cliff lift, which links the promenade with Scarborough Spa, is the oldest funicular railway in the country. It originally ran on a hydraulic system using gas engines and seawater.

Scarborough train station is back up the hill above the South Bay.

APPENDIX A
Accommodation

Location	Type	Name	Phone	Website or email	Evening meal available	En route	Bike storage
Morecambe	Hotel	Crown	01524 831841	thecrownhotelmorecambe.co.uk	Yes	Yes	Yes
Morecambe	Art deco hotel	Midland	01524 424000	englishlakes.co.uk	Yes	Yes	
Morecambe	B&B	Clifton	01524 411573	hotel-clifton.co.uk		Yes	Yes
Morecambe	B&B	Craigwell	01524 410095	craigwellhotel.co.uk		Yes	Yes
Morecambe	B&B	Wimslow	01524 417804	thewimslow.co.uk		Yes	Yes
Bolton-le-Sands	Camping	Red Bank Farm	01524 832198	redbankfarm.co.uk		4 miles away	
Lancaster	Hotel	Royal Kings Arms	01524 32451	royalkingsarmshotel.co.uk	Yes	¼ mile away	
Lancaster	Pub	Wagon and Horses	01524 846094	wagonandhorseslancaster.co.uk	Yes	Yes	Yes limited
Lancaster	Pub	Sun	01524 66006	thesunhotelandbar.co.uk	Yes	Yes	By arrangement
Lancaster	University guest rooms	University	01524 592899	lancaster.ac.uk/conferences		2 miles away	
Caton	Camping	New Parkside Farm	01524 770723			1 mile away	
Crook o' Lune	Scarthwaite	Hotel	01524 770267	thescarthwaite.co.uk	Yes	Yes	

Location	Type	Name	Phone	Website or email	Evening meal available	En route	Bike storage
Clapham	Bunkhouse	Clapham bunkhouse	01524 251144	claphambunk.com	Yes	Yes	Yes
Clapham	B&B	Brookhouse guest house	01524 251580	brookhouse-clapham.co.uk	Yes	Yes	
Austwick	B&B, bunkhouse, camping	Dalesbridge Centre	01524 251021	dalesbridge.co.uk		1 mile away	Yes
Austwick	Hotel	Traddock	01524 251224	thetraddock.co.uk	Yes	Yes	
Austwick	Camping	Silloth House	07854 368832	silloth-house.co.uk		Yes	
Helwith Bridge, Settle	Bunkhouse	YSS bunkhouse	01729 860318	yssuk.com	pub nearby	Yes	Yes
Helwith Bridge, Settle	Inn, small bunkhouse, camping	Helwith Bridge Inn	01729 860220	helwithbridgeinn.co.uk	Yes	Yes	
Stainforth, Settle	B&B	Holly House	01729 823876	hollyhousestainforth.co.uk	pub nearby	Yes	
Giggleswick, Settle	Hotel	Harts Head	01729 822086	hartsheadhotel.co.uk	Yes	Yes	Yes
Giggleswick, Settle	B&B	Valleymead	01729 822386	settle-b-b.co.uk		Yes	Yes
Settle	B&B	King William IV	01729 268152	kingwilliamthefourthguest-house.co.uk		Yes	Yes
Settle	B&B	Settle Lodge	01729 823259	settlelodge.co.uk		Yes	

Location	Type	Name	Phone	Website or email	Evening meal available	En route	Bike storage
Airton	Bunkhouse	Airton barn	01729 830263	airtonbarn.co.uk	pre-order farm shop takeaway	Yes	Yes
Airton	B&B	Lindon	01729 830418	lindonguesthouse.co.uk	pre-order	Yes	Yes
Cracoe	Inn	Devonshire Arms	01756 73237	devonshirearmsinn.co.uk	Yes	Yes	Yes
Cracoe	B&B	Brookside Cottage	01756 730338	cracoebandb.co.uk	pub nearby	Yes	Yes
Burnsall	Bunkhouse	Burnsall village hall	01756 720680	burnsallvillagehall.org.uk	pub nearby	Yes	
Burnsall	B&B	Wharfe View Farm	01756 720643	burnsall.net	pub nearby	Yes	Yes
Burnsall	Inn/B&B	Red Lion	01756 720204	redlion.co.uk	Yes	Yes	Yes
Burnsall	Hotel	Devonshire Fell	01756 729000	devonshirefell.co.uk	Yes	½ mile away	
Burnsall	B&B	Raikes Acre	01756 720206	raikesacre.co.uk		½ mile away	
Appletreewick	Camping, pods, rent a tent	Masons	01756 720275	masonscampsite.co.uk	pub nearby	Yes	
Appletreewick	Inn	New Inn	01756 720252	the-new-inn-appletree-wick.com	Yes	Yes	Yes
Appletreewick	Shepherd huts	Craven Arms	01756 720270	craven-cruckbarn.co.uk	Yes	Yes	
Greenhow	B&B	East Wayside	01423 313142	eastwayside.co.uk	free transport to town	Yes	Yes
Greenhow	B&B	Fancarl House	01756 752753	email annemitt43@gmail.com	transport to pub	Yes	Yes

Location	Type	Name	Phone	Website or email	Evening meal available	En route	Bike storage
Pateley Bridge/ Bewerley	Group dorm	Bewerley Park	01423 711287	email nyols@northyorks. gov.uk		Yes	Yes
Pateley Bridge	B&B	Roslyn House	01423 711374	roslynhouse.co.uk		Yes	
Pateley Bridge	B&B	Lyndale	01423 712657	lyndaleguesthouse.com	nearby	Yes	Yes
Pateley Bridge	Hotel, bunkhouse	Harefield Hall	01423 711429	harefieldhall.com	Yes	Yes	Yes
Pateley Bridge	B&B	Talbot	01423 711597	talbothouse.co.uk	nearby	Yes	Yes
Studley Roger, Ripon	Camping, shepherd's hut, tree-house, guest room	Jelley Legs	01765 603506	jelleylegs.co.uk	Yes	Yes	Yes
Ripon	B&B	Kangel Corner	01765 602285	email phillipaoates@hot-mail.com		Yes	Yes
Ripon	Camping	Lockside, Littlethorpe Road	01765 605117			Yes	
Ripon	B&B	Ship Inn	01765 451562	theshipinnripon.co.uk	nearby	Yes	Yes
Ripon	B&B	Crescent Lodge	01765 451562	crescent-lodge.com	nearby	Yes	
Bishop Monkton	Barns	Mill View Barns	01765 677334	millviewbarns.com	nearby	Yes	Yes
Bishop Monkton	Barn at pub	Lamb and Flag	01765 677322	lambandflagbarn.co.uk	Yes	Yes	
Boroughbridge	Inn	Black Bull	01423 322413	blackbullboroughbridge. co.uk	Yes	Yes	
Boroughbridge	Inn	Grantham Arms	01423 323980	granthamarms.co.uk	Yes	Yes	

Location	Type	Name	Phone	Website or email	Evening meal available	En route	Bike storage
Skelton, York	Camping	Grantchester	07472 694380	grantchestercamping.co.uk	nearby	Yes	
York	Youth hostel	York YHA	0345 371 9051	yha.org.uk	Yes	Yes	Yes
York	Hostel	Stableside, racecourse	01904 709174	stablesideyork.co.uk		Yes	Yes
York	B&B	Gillygate	01904 654103	gillygateyork.co.uk	Yes	Yes	Yes
York	B&B	St Marys guest house	01904 626972				
York	B&B	Hazelwood	01904 626548	thehazelwoodyork.com		Yes	
York	B&B	Bloomsbury	01904 634031	thebloomsburyguesthouse.com		Yes	Yes
Dunnington	Inn	Windmill	01904 481898	thewindmilldunnington.co.uk	Yes	Yes	
Holtby, Dunnington	Glamping pods	York cycle stop	07834 257985	yorkcyclestop.co.uk	nearby	1 mile away	Yes
Stamford Bridge	B&B, group room	Birkhouse	01759 529054	birkhousebandb.wixsite.com/birkhouse-save	nearby	½ mile away	
Pocklington	Camping	Mile Farm	01759 305420	themilefarmshop.co.uk	½ mile away	Yes	
Pocklington	B&B	Meltonby villas	01759 302429	meltonbyvillas.co.uk	nearby	Yes	Yes
Pocklington	B&B	Ashfield Farm	01759 305238		nearby	Yes	
Pocklington	Inn	The Feathers	01759 303155	thefeatherspocklington.co.uk	Yes	Yes	Yes
Kilnwick Percy	B&B/retreat	Wolds Retreat	01759 304832	thewoldsretreat.co.uk	Yes	Yes	
Millington	B&B	Laburnum Cottage	01759 303055	millingtonbandb.co.uk	nearby	Yes	

Location	Type	Name	Phone	Website or email	Evening meal available	En route	Bike storage
Millington	Inn	Ramblers Rest	01759 305220	ramblersrestmillington.co.uk	Yes	Yes	
Millington	Dorm	Village Hall	01759 304735	millingtonvillagehall.org.uk	nearby	Yes	
Huggate	Inn and camping	Wolds Inn	01377 288217	woldsinn.co.uk	Yes	Yes	
Southburn, Driffield	B&B	Highfield Farm	01377 227723	highfieldfarm.co.uk	Yes	Yes	Yes
Nafferton	Bunk barn	Nether Lane	01377 241711	email annetteatnether-lane@live.co.uk	nearby	Yes	Yes
Bridlington	B&B	Swandale	01262 603966	swandaleguesthouse.co.uk	Yes	Yes	Yes
Bridlington	B&B	South Lodge	01262 671040	southlodge-bridlington.co.uk		Yes	Yes
Bridlington	B&B	Malvern	01262 679695	malvernguesthousebri-dlington.co.uk		Yes	Yes
Flamborough	B&B	Manor House	01262 850943	flamboroughmanor.co.uk	nearby	alt finish	Yes
Flamborough	Camping/pods	Wold Farm	01262 850536	woldfarmcampsite.com	nearby	alt finish	

167

APPENDIX B
Useful contacts

Bike shops in route order

Morecambe
Smalleys
104 Euston Road
LA4 5LD
01524 412446

Lancaster
The Edge Cycleworks
2 Chapel Street
LA1 1NZ
01524 840800
www.theedgecycleworks.com

Leisure Lakes Bikes
103–105 Penny Street
LA1 1XN
01524 844389
www.leisurelakesbikes.com

Settle
3 Peaks Cycles
Market Place
BD24 9EJ
01729 824232
www.3peakscycles.com

Appletreewick
Mountain Bike Livery
behind the New Inn
BD23 6DA
01756 720319

Pateley Bridge
Stif Cycles
New York Mills
Summerbridge
HG3 4LA
01423 780738

(1¼ miles off route)
www.stif.co.uk

Ripon
Moonglu
57 Blossomgate
HG4 2AN
01765 601106
www.moonglu.com

Boroughbridge
Karbitz
33 High Street
YO51 9AW
01423 324085

York
York Cycleworks
4–16 Lawrence Street
YO10 3WP
01904 626664
www.yorkcycleworks.com

Cycle Heaven
York train station
YO24 1AY
01904 622701
www.cycle-heaven.co.uk

CycleStreet
87 Layerthorpe
YO31 7UZ
01904 655063
www.cycle-street.co.uk

Pocklington
CycleLane
6 Clarkes Lane
YO42 2AW
01759 306770
www.cyclelane-ltd.co.uk

Driffield
The Bike Cave
36 Market Place
YO25 6AR
01377 232736
www.thebikecavedriffield.co.uk

East Gate Cycles
Eastgate
YO25 6EB
01377 253274
www.eastgatecycles.com

Bridlington
Chaiin Cycles
133 Hilderthorpe Road
YO15 3EX
01262 677555
www.chaiincycles.co.uk

Useful for the day rides
Skipton – Chevin Cycles
11 High Street
BD23 1AA
0800 023 4146
www.chevincycles.com

Otley – Chevin Cycles
Gay Lane
LS21 1BR
0800 023 4146
www.chevincycles.com

Malton – Northern Ride
19 Saville Street
YO17 7LL
01653 699070
www.northernride.com

Scarborough – Richardson's Cycles
38–40 Castle Road
YO11 1XE
01723 352682
richardsonscyclesscarborough.co.uk

Cycle transport
Carry on Cycling
07969 119064
info@bridcars.co.uk

Pedal Power
01665 713448/07790 596782
www.pedal-power.co.uk

Sherwoods
01765 635262
www.sherwoodsminibus.co.uk

Yorkshire Cycle Transfers
01964 544131, 07778 693870
www.yorkshirecycletransfers.co.uk

Yorkshire Dales Media Group
01729 830463/07766 894529
info@wayoftheroses.co.uk

Companies that arrange accommodation and transport as a package
Brigantes
01756 770402
www.brigantesenglishwalks.com

CycleActive
01768 840400
www.cycleactive.com

Inspiring Cycling
07887 764987
www.inspiringcycling.co.uk

Peak Tours
01457 851462
www.peak-tours.com

Trailbrakes
01416 286676/ 07922 653327
www.trailbrakes.co.uk

The toughest test of the ride –High Hill Lane out of Settle. Note the zigzagging cyclist behind (Day 1)

DOWNLOAD THE ROUTE IN GPX FORMAT

All the routes in this guide are available for download from:

www.cicerone.co.uk/912/GPX

as GPX files. You should be able to load them into most formats of mobile device, whether GPS or smartphone.

When you go to this link, you will be asked for your email address and where you purchased the guide, and have the option to subscribe to the Cicerone e-newsletter.

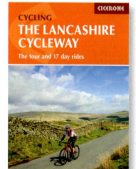
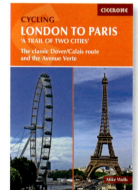

LISTING OF CICERONE GUIDES

SCOTLAND

Backpacker's Britain:
    Northern Scotland
Ben Nevis and Glen Coe
Cycling in the Hebrides
Great Mountain Days in Scotland
Mountain Biking in Southern and
    Central Scotland
Mountain Biking in West and
    North West Scotland
Not the West Highland Way
Scotland
Scotland's Best Small Mountains
Scotland's Far West
Scotland's Mountain Ridges
Scrambles in Lochaber
The Ayrshire and Arran
    Coastal Paths
The Border Country
The Cape Wrath Trail
The Great Glen Way
The Great Glen Way Map Booklet
The Hebridean Way
The Hebrides
The Isle of Mull
The Isle of Skye
The Skye Trail
The Southern Upland Way
The Speyside Way
The Speyside Way Map Booklet
The West Highland Way
Walking Highland Perthshire
Walking in Scotland's Far North
Walking in the Angus Glens
Walking in the Cairngorms
Walking in the Ochils, Campsie
    Fells and Lomond Hills
Walking in the Pentland Hills
Walking in the Southern Uplands
Walking in Torridon
Walking Loch Lomond and
    the Trossachs
Walking on Arran
Walking on Harris and Lewis
Walking on Jura, Islay
    and Colonsay
Walking on Rum and the
    Small Isles
Walking on the Orkney and
    Shetland Isles
Walking on Uist and Barra
Walking the Corbetts Vol 1
Walking the Corbetts Vol 2
Walking the Galloway Hills
Walking the Munros Vol 1
Walking the Munros Vol 2
West Highland Way Map Booklet

Winter Climbs Ben Nevis and
    Glen Coe
Winter Climbs in the Cairngorms

NORTHERN ENGLAND TRAILS

Hadrian's Wall Path
Hadrian's Wall Path Map Booklet
Pennine Way Map Booklet
The Coast to Coast Walk
The Coast to Coast Map Booklet
The Dales Way
The Pennine Way

LAKE DISTRICT

Cycling in the Lake District
Great Mountain Days in the
    Lake District
Lake District Winter Climbs
Lake District:
    High Level and Fell Walks
Lake District:
    Low Level and Lake Walks
Lakeland Fellranger
Mountain Biking in the
    Lake District
Scafell Pike
Scrambles in the Lake District
    – North
Scrambles in the Lake District
    – South
Short Walks in Lakeland
    Book 1: South Lakeland
Short Walks in Lakeland
    Book 2: North Lakeland
Short Walks in Lakeland
    Book 3: West Lakeland
Tour of the Lake District
Trail and Fell Running in the
    Lake District

NORTH WEST ENGLAND
AND THE ISLE OF MAN

Cycling the Pennine Bridleway
Isle of Man Coastal Path
The Lancashire Cycleway
The Lune Valley and Howgills
The Ribble Way
Walking in Cumbria's Eden Valley
Walking in Lancashire
Walking in the Forest of Bowland
    and Pendle
Walking on the Isle of Man
Walking on the West
    Pennine Moors
Walks in Lancashire
    Witch Country
Walks in Ribble Country
Walks in Silverdale and Arnside

NORTH EAST ENGLAND,
YORKSHIRE DALES
AND PENNINES

Cycling in the Yorkshire Dales
Great Mountain Days in
    the Pennines
Historic Walks in North Yorkshire
Mountain Biking in the
    Yorkshire Dales
South Pennine Walks
St Oswald's Way and
    St Cuthbert's Way
The Cleveland Way and the
    Yorkshire Wolds Way
The Cleveland Way Map Booklet
The North York Moors
The Reivers Way
The Teesdale Way
Walking in County Durham
Walking in Northumberland
Walking in the North Pennines
Walking in the Yorkshire Dales:
    North and East
Walking in the Yorkshire Dales:
    South and West
Walks in Dales Country
Walks in the Yorkshire Dales

WALES AND WELSH BORDERS

Glyndwr's Way
Great Mountain Days
    in Snowdonia
Hillwalking in Shropshire
Hillwalking in Wales – Vol 1
Hillwalking in Wales – Vol 2
Mountain Walking in Snowdonia
Offa's Dyke Path
Offa's Dyke Map Booklet
Pembrokeshire Coast Path
    Map Booklet
Ridges of Snowdonia
Scrambles in Snowdonia
The Ascent of Snowdon
The Ceredigion and Snowdonia
    Coast Paths
The Pembrokeshire Coast Path
The Severn Way
The Snowdonia Way
The Wales Coast Path
The Wye Valley Walk
Walking in Carmarthenshire
Walking in Pembrokeshire
Walking in the Forest of Dean
Walking in the South
    Wales Valleys
Walking in the Wye Valley
Walking on the Brecon Beacons

For full information on all our
guides, books and eBooks,
visit our website:
www.cicerone.co.uk

Walking – Trekking – Mountaineering – Climbing – Cycling

Over 40 years, Cicerone have built up an outstanding collection of over 300 guides, inspiring all sorts of amazing adventures.

 Every guide comes from extensive exploration and research by our expert authors, all with a passion for their subjects. They are frequently praised, endorsed and used by clubs, instructors and outdoor organisations.

All our titles can now be bought as **e-books**, **ePubs** and **Kindle** files and we also have an online magazine – **Cicerone Extra** – with features to help cyclists, climbers, walkers and trekkers choose their next adventure, at home or abroad.

Our website shows any **new information** we've had in since a book was published. Please do let us know if you find anything has changed, so that we can publish the latest details. On our **website** you'll also find great ideas and lots of detailed information about what's inside every guide and you can buy **individual routes** from many of them online.

It's easy to keep in touch with what's going on at Cicerone by getting our monthly **free e-newsletter**, which is full of offers, competitions, up-to-date information and topical articles. You can subscribe on our home page and also follow us on **Facebook** and **Twitter** or dip into our **blog**.

Cicerone – the very best guides for exploring the world.

CICERONE

Juniper House, Murley Moss, Oxenholme Road, Kendal, Cumbria LA9 7RL
Tel: 015395 62069 info@cicerone.co.uk
www.cicerone.co.uk